Living in the Zone

Dan and Suzi Fiedler

Trilogy Christian Publishers
A Wholly Owned Subsidiary of Trinity Broadcasting Network
2442 Michelle Drive
Tustin, CA 92780

For information, address Trilogy Christian Publishing
Rights Department, 2442 Michelle Drive, Tustin, Ca 92780.
Trilogy Christian Publishing/ TBN and colophon are trademarks of Trinity Broadcasting Network.

For information about special discounts for bulk purchases, please contact Trilogy Christian Publishing.

Manufactured in the United States of America

10 9 8 7 6 5 4 3 2 1

Library of Congress Cataloging-in-Publication Data is available.

ISBN 978-1-64773-760-3 (Print Book)
ISBN 978-1-64773-761-0 (ebook)

We would like to dedicate this book most assuredly to Jesus.
Our thinking would be a mess, and so would our lives,
without God putting forth His Word to us as a guide
in how to think, what to think, and what to say.

Contents

Foreword

from some whoevers

> But whoever takes a drink of the water that I will give him shall never, no never, be thirsty any more. But the water that I will give him shall become a spring of water welling up (flowing, bubbling) [continually] within him unto (into, for) eternal life. (John 4:14 AMPC)

I so enjoyed the book! I found it very encouraging. There are a couple of chapters that rocked my world, and in fact, I read them over and over. I realized how many of these principles I had not considered in some years. At that point, I found myself somewhat excited about the future. I'd become stoically stagnant, especially in regards to concerns about any financial potential. I'm encouraged that the author reminds the reader not to skip over reading the Scriptures.

—Rick Priem

This book touched my life in so many ways, and I want that for others too. It was so good I'm getting it out and reading it over again. The reader will be inspired by the author's stories as they make you laugh and make you look at yourself in a way that humbles you to strive to be a better person. This is a book that will not only make you love God more but also encourage you to go deeper with Him.

—Ken and Kathy Vorpahl

We so enjoyed reading this book because whether you want to know how to live in the secret place, practice the presence of God, or hear the voice of God, it is contained in these wonderful examples in the life of one believer.

—Dave and Debbie Fiedler

Living in the Zone describes a life that is lived by faith in Jesus Christ. As I read this book, I became more aware of God's presence as I spend time in His Word and listen to His voice. This book reminded me of my part in His master plan to draw all people to Himself.

—Laura Barr Walker

This book was truly inspiring. People go through life never learning how to grow in their relationship with God or learn how to build on their level of faith. This book will challenge you through testimonies and scriptures on how to have a deeper relationship with Christ so you can be that tree planted by the river's edge.

—Julie and Bryan Maloney

The book you are holding in your hands is filled with true stories that speak wisdom and encouragement into your life. If you let it, this book has the power to change your life in ways that you will never be the same nor ever want to be the same again.

—Ken Vorpahl

My longtime friend, Dan Fiedler, has revelation that very few people possess. It's not for a specific God-given calling but rather a wisdom to rely on and follow the Holy Spirit regarding extraordinary wealth and finances, which are used to advance God's kingdom. The insight in this book will make you laugh and provoke you to deepen your sensitivity to godly ways of giving and receiving.

Together, Dan and Suzi walk in this anointing and want to share these principles with us. I'm so grateful that this timely Word is getting out for such a time as this!

—Joe Firestone

Acknowledgments

We would like to thank all the people who have gone before us, gone with us, influenced us, and helped make us better, stronger Christians. Thank God for books! We have learned so much from those who have handed down their wisdom via their writings.

Also, we would like to thank Chuck Ramsey, Suzi's brother, for his tedious hours in being the first editor of the book and, within that, being the first reader. He sure is a smart guy, and we are thankful for his ever-agreeable assistance in this undertaking.

Lastly, we would like to thank Mom (Mildred Rose Fiedler) for praying for all her kids for so many years. We know she is running on streets of gold! She would have liked this book.

Introduction

This book is for the average person who wants to accomplish great things in their life. For it is the average, natural person who would be able to do the supernatural. And it is the ordinary one who can do the extraordinary. This is what Jesus says:

> I assure you, most solemnly I tell you, if anyone steadfastly believes in Me, he will himself be able to do the things that I do; and he will do even greater things than these, because I go to the Father. (John 14:12 AMPC)

It's amazing, truly amazing, what can happen when you really believe the Word of God.

1
The Reason: Is There Not a Cause?

We drift through life sometimes not realizing how many godly systems are in place. They are working without our awareness, but they're there for us to use, if only we would. I hope to expose some of these systems to you so that you can take advantage of them and make your life better. That's the reason for the book: to make your life better by revealing information you never realized.

Did you ever wonder how many times a twenty-dollar bill nestled in leaves by a drain cover may have been walked past and overlooked before *you* found it? Certainly, others would have bent down to pick it up had they known it was there. Or did you ever put on a pair of pants and find a $20 bill in the pocket that you had forgotten about? Information is like that. It's there for us, but do we know about it?

It is information that begins the process of change in us. And change is good. God says His people die because they just don't know! We need to embrace knowledge. Always.

Be sure to read the boxes in this book, for they contain that all-important knowledge.

> My people are destroyed for lack of knowledge. (Hosea 4:6a AMP)

What's the reason for the title of the book? In football, there is the red zone. It's the twenty yards before the opponent's end zone, where, if the ball crosses, you score. It is said of players who experience a good game that they were "in the zone" that night. They were in the right place, at the right time, doing the right thing. A rookie barely knows what the zone is about, but I can guarantee that the first touchdown he scores, he keeps that football. How does it feel when you score? It's a conquering, blissful, euphoric feeling!

I have a phrase I commonly say to my wife to let her know God is speaking to me. I say, "I'm in the zone right now." There are those occasions where my time with Him is especially clear and informative. My goal is to live in the zone, as much as I can. My desire is to be in tune with Him and His direction in my life. With God on my side, I've scored many times.

Early in my Christian walk, I felt I was given marching orders to get up at 5:00 a.m. and pray for an hour. That yearlong commitment changed my life forever. After some months, I was hooked into a rhythm of the system of tapping into the Spirit of God and listening to that still small voice. Since then, I have had such specific words from God that it could only be attributed *to* God. My thought at that time became an ongoing prayer, "Lord, show me what I need to see, what others don't see."

I remember exactly one of the first times I heard the voice of God in a specific way. I was a builder and was building my wife's and my first log home. I had leaned my four-foot level against the wall. If you know anything about levels, that bubble that sits between two lines had better be calibrated correctly, or you will have walls resembling a house of cards. I had a sudden inkling that I should lay the level down. I didn't. Then yet another passing thought: *Move the level.* Again, I didn't. Three seconds later, there it went. I had turned away, heard a sliding sound and a loud clap. My outstretched hand was too late to grab the level as it fell to the floor.

That single miniscule event changed me. The level was valuable, but more valuable was what I took away from that moment in time. Why didn't I just listen to that little inkling inside me? Now I know how, how to "live in the zone," hearing God's direction.

> And he said, Go forth, and stand upon the mount before the Lord. And, behold, the Lord passed by, and a great and strong wind rent the mountains, and brake in pieces the rocks before the Lord; but the Lord was not in the wind: and after the wind an earthquake; but the Lord was not in the earthquake: And after the earthquake a fire; but the Lord was not in the fire: and after the fire *a still small voice.* (1 Kings 19:11–12 KJV)

That's how information comes. It's little. It's a sentence, a brief experience, or a "learning," if you will. It can be short and quick. For me, many times it's just a single word. It could be a small happening like the level incident that grabs your attention for some reason. Sometimes you don't know its significance at that time, but eventually you figure it out. And the lesson learned sticks with you, if you will pay attention to it. That is, if you desire to live in the zone. Isn't that how the Word of God is learned? Little by little?

> For precept must be upon precept, precept upon precept; line upon line, line upon line; here a little, and there a little. (Isa. 28:10 KJV)

I've had many accurate leadings from the Spirit of God, some of which you'll read in this book, but I would say the most bizarre example was when I had a bit of a busy morning but most distinctly heard the Lord say inside me, "Would you like some jewelry?" I battled with the usual thoughts: *What? Where did that thought come from? Is that You, Lord? What do You mean exactly? Where? I'm kinda busy.* And on and on with the self-doubt thoughts that can drive us more than God's voice.

But I drove past my place of work, past my 9:00 a.m. meeting, and past rational thinking. I went in my truck, as instructed, to the edge of a mountain of snow in a Sam's Club parking lot. Though it was only a short distance from work, the entire way I wondered if I had really lost it. Had anyone been in the truck with me, I certainly wouldn't have shared with them what I was about to do. This had nothing to do with common sense. There wasn't an ounce of logic in this time-stealing plan. You look for jewelry at home on a dresser or in the store at the jewelry counter, not in a snowbank! Nevertheless, I slowly drove along that great wall of snow, looking out the window at the melting edge. Within a few feet of commencing, I saw something that looked like a noodle. I got out and, lo and behold, picked up a small marquis diamond ring in the water. I put it in my coffee cup holder and drove away. Talk about finding a needle in a haystack!

In shock, I pulled over after a minute and said to myself, "Wow! What just happened? The God who knows me and talks to me knows *everything* else. He knows everything! If I can listen, I can get direction to and for everything in my life." I was so thrilled at the pinpoint precision of hearing the voice of my Father that I drove off half-dumbfounded, half-awed. This opened a whole new world to me in trusting what I hear and know to be true. The incident with the level many years before was commonsense. Lesson learned: Don't lean a level against the wall. Lay it down. That makes sense. The jewelry incident made no sense. You might be thinking, "Why did you stop with the diamond ring find? Why not look for more?" I was in a state of shock as it was and didn't even consider that there might be more. I was elated with what I drove away with—more knowledge. I scored. I was in the zone for a moment in time.

In my life, I've had many such happenings and have honed the listening art tremendously. That's not something you want to make a mistake on, as it can cost you more than a level that isn't level. I love the zone. I crave it. It's a place of harmony and one of peace. It's a place of clarity, a place of information. You bring a piece of heaven to your life. It's like grabbing a star. I mean, it's that big.

Now I knew firsthand the power and the feeling inside of these scriptures:

> For wisdom is far more valuable than rubies. Nothing you desire can compare with it. (Prov. 8:11 NLT)
>
> The kingdom of heaven is like something precious buried in a field, which a man found and hid again; then in his joy he goes and sells all he has and buys that field. (Matt. 13:44 NLT)

I wondered if I should tell anyone of this diamond ring incident. Would they even believe me? I have kept that ring as confirmation that God does indeed desire to speak plainly and distinctly to me and reveal secrets. And I believe He even has fun doing it! But He will not impose Himself upon me if I am not willing. God is ultimately developing trust. Can He trust me? And will I trust Him?

Trust. It's like someone who desires to tame a wild kitten they've seen hanging around outside. You start with setting out food. Then you set out the food and leave the light on. Then you allow your presence to be seen in the window, watching the kitten as it approaches. With patience, you sit outside as the kitten eats. Soon Kitty is on your lap while you watch TV and has become your house pet. That's how it works. Now the cat knows where its bread is buttered. With God, trust is a process. It's developed over time. Now, for me, life has never been more fun, knowing where my bread is buttered. And I truly know this scripture from experience:

> My heart has heard you say, "Come and talk with me." And my heart responds, "Lord, I am coming." (Ps. 27:8 NLT)

2
Truth: It's Always in Season

Reminder: Don't skip reading the scriptures in the boxes. They're the best part of the book, because they're to the point and say it all.

Subsequent to the practice of giving my initial thoughts and attention to God and His Word, even before my eyes open to begin a new day, I've heard of a wealthy businessman's daily practice. He dedicates his success to sitting every morning, observing how God does things in nature. The man then duplicates the systems that he sees from God's view in his own business ventures. What a concept! I decided to try this observation process myself.

It wasn't hard. We lived overlooking a beautiful wooded area at that time. I observed much there, and then we moved to a house we built on a lake. This afforded a vast new encyclopedia of knowledge about godly systems in place in nature. The lessons learned there are amazing to me to this day.

God teaches me His principles, at times using these visual examples found in nature. The Bible says that nature itself bears witness to the glory of God. I believe the systems present in nature also bear witness to the wisdom of God.

> The heavens proclaim the glory of God. The skies display his craftsmanship. Day after day they continue to speak; night after night they make him known. They speak without a sound or word; their voice is never heard. (Ps. 19:1–3 NLT)

Remember my prayer? "Lord, show me what others don't see." Here's the thing: you've got to *look* for what you don't see. God's wisdom and way of doing things are always in season. Once you see it, it becomes louder than anything else around you. Then you know you're in the zone. It's enlightenment. It brings focus. It's a flashlight showing the way for you on a dark night.

> Your word is a lamp to guide my feet and a light for my path. (Ps. 119:105 NLT)
>
> By your words I can see where I'm going; they throw a beam of light on my dark path. (Ps. 119:105 MSG)

The biggest illusion of life is seeing what everyone else sees. Often, it's the problem. It's part of the needs, wants, fleshly desires, and fears that try to rule us. The crowd goes in a particular direction, so surely, that must be the correct way to go, right? The best example of this is from Moses in Numbers chapters 13 and 14. Of the twelve spies sent out to report on the new land God had given to them, it was Joshua and Caleb who were commended for *not* going the way of the crowd. Everyone saw that the giants in the land were too big. How could the Israelites possibly succeed against them? They weren't battle-hardened warriors. But those two gentlemen only saw God and how big *He* is. I believe they had to be looking for what the others just couldn't see. After all, seeing is *not* believing. Believing is seeing.

My premise with this book is that we can learn lessons by viewing nature and the systems that God has in place to help us and take care of us. I'll share with you the truths (principles) I've learned by observing nature and also by personal practice. Now they're so obvious to me.

Jesus used comparisons to nature all the time. He called them parables.

> They know the truth about God because He has made it obvious to them. For ever since the world was created, people have seen the earth and sky. Through everything God made, they can clearly see His invisible qualities—His eternal power and divine nature. So they have no excuse for not knowing God. (Rom. 1:20–21 NLT)

Soil, seed, vines, branches, water, nutrients, mulch, fruit, harvest, and their operations are all so clearly comparable to needed principles for life. I may repeat principles and scriptures in the book, but if you know anything about learning, repetition is key.

God implores us in Luke 12:27 to consider lilies. Sometimes "living" is a little easier than we think. We complicate it; we add difficulties by wanting things that aren't necessary for happiness. Then we skip over the things that would bring us great joy. What a condition!

> Look at the lilies and how they grow. They don't work or make their clothing, yet Solomon in all his glory was not dressed as beautifully as they are. (Luke 12:27 NLT)

Leaves: Lesson 1 from the Tree

I received a revelation from God as I looked out my window at a huge maple tree and considered its method of operation. Its leaves' purpose is to collect sunshine. They bask in the sun and turn whichever way is needed to follow the sun. A canopy of leaves develops because every leaf is performing its function of stretching to absorb that sunshine. We call it photosynthesis, but it's comparable to us eating a grilled cheese. The tree eats sunshine. It eats nutrients from the soil where it's living, and drinks water.

Leaves produce what's needed for the season and then drop to the forest floor, where they dissolve or decompose. It's a cycle, one of many God has established. The leaves produce everything for the tree, but the tree forms the leaves. If you prematurely remove all of a tree's leaves, it goes into struggle mode. The majority of its focus will be to get those leaves in place again. It's the lifeblood for that growing season.

Here's the principle: If I were a tree, my leaves would be my words. I speak, and those words fall and are heard by my own ears—every one of them. I create the words, but the words I speak enrich and form me. Well, hopefully they're words that enrich and do not destroy. My trunk can draw from those words that are spoken. That richly mulched soil from leaves that have dropped to the base of the tree feeds the tree. A mighty elm tree's leaf is so small compared to the trunk, yet with so many, the tree grows strong and tall. One might think the trunk is the life giver, but it's the little leaves that *produce* that tree.

It's like a river. The banks hold the river, but the river forms the banks. The Word of God forms you, as those words are believed and go back into you when you speak them. They empower you to grow and produce. When you're new at this and you read some scripture that you can't believe, say the words out loud anyway and you *will* come to believe them after a time. Their truth will come to light. You'll find out why in the next scripture box.

When I met my wife-to-be, she had trouble believing the Bible. She would say, "It is, after all, a book that is over two thousand years old. How could it possibly have relevance in today's world?" She didn't take my word for it but asked her brother, who she knew was a believer. He had a simple answer to her question of, "How can you believe that a bunch of animals just walked into a prepared boat and sailed off safely? Even if they could fit on one boat, how did Noah gather them all up?" He told her, "If you believe that God is a God of miracles, then He can do anything. It was a miracle. That's all." That was it for her. She started reading the Bible for herself to find out what it contained. A short time later, she gave her heart and belief system over to Jesus and has been growing ever since that day.

Just like she came to believe what she read from the Bible as true, we all need to do the same. When it comes to a Bible in your hands, the words are not just words on a page; they're alive because they're inspired by God, and He is the ultimate giver of life.

> For the Word that God speaks is alive and full of power [making it active, operative, energizing, and effective]; it is sharper than any two-edged sword, penetrating to the dividing line of the breath of life (soul) and [the immortal] spirit, and of joints and marrow [of the deepest parts of our nature], exposing and sifting and analyzing and judging the very thoughts and purposes of the heart. (Heb. 4:12 AMPC)

If you're a seasoned Christian, you know that words are powerful. They are one of the greatest tools on this earth.

Children come to understand words very fast. When they're only a year into our world, they're learning the system. The brain is an amazing, complex, yet simple device that God has given for our use.

Our words are forming us every day. We pick from our words every waking moment. They're making us, or breaking us. If our words are formed from our thinking because we've been bathing in the *Sonlight* of the Bible, then they are seasoned with the spices of God and are tasty and nutritious. If our words are void of God's Word, then they lack the nutrients and flavor we need to become strong and productive. Earthly pleasures can come to leave us dry, and we become unenthused, sometimes even to the point of wanting to end it all.

I've known a sincere older gentleman named Jerry since my younger years with a last name that is fifteen letters long and ends in *ski*. When we met, he would speak but seemingly talk in circles. It was difficult to follow what he was trying to get across. He would end his stories with, "I'm sorry, you probably don't understand me. I'm just a dumb Pollock." After some time, I decided to challenge his method of operation. Looking for what others don't see, I felt that God wanted me to have a chat with him and suggest that he never use the phrase "I'm just a dumb Pollock" again. I met with him and explained why.

He grabbed that advice and almost instantly changed! His speech became coherent, and his stories followed a path that others could follow too. It was almost as if he squared back his shoulders, stood a little taller, and decided that he was worthy to be listened to. He stopped drinking his own poison. As time went on, he became a well-respected man in his church, with his family and friends and, most importantly, with himself. The river had been rerouted. By his changing his words, his tree began to produce fruit that others could pick. Such a small adjustment began the process of change in him.

> So here's what I want you to do, God helping you: Take your everyday, ordinary life—your sleeping, eating, going-to-work, and walking-around life—and place it before God as an offering. Embracing what God does for you is the best thing you can do for Him. Don't become so well-adjusted to your culture that you fit into it without even thinking. Instead, fix your attention on God. You'll be changed from the inside out. Readily recognize what He wants from you, and quickly respond to it. Unlike the culture around you, always dragging you down to its level of immaturity, God brings the best out of you, develops well-formed maturity in you. (Rom. 12:1–2 MSG)

Our friend Jerry became resourceful, helpful, giving, and loved by many. Of course, he always was valuable to God. He just didn't know it for himself or believe it.

Is there something you say continually that you know is taking you down a wrong road? You may not think you're an addict, but you are. You're drugged with your own thoughts, and they're killing you. You would steal a TV from your loving mother to support your "habit." Drug addicts can develop an infected arm and subsequent amputation and still shoot up. They have no power over that which is destroying them. Their thoughts are linked to an accompanying emotion, and that's why they're hooked. Your thoughts become words and attitudes that infect those around you. If your loved ones don't know the antidote, they become part of the problem. Speak over that addiction mountain! Disclaim its power to take your sleep.

A river is not harnessed for power until it's narrowed. Do you have tributaries that need to be cut off? Is your river so wide that it's become as shallow as a puddle, with the inability to produce anything but muddy water? Do you really have something to say, or do you just have to say something?

When you speak the Word of God and come to believe it deep on the inside, the banks of your river come closer. You gain focus in life. Your leaves are photosynthesizing at the optimum level because it's a sunny day. You have a pile of leaves at the base of your trunk from which to draw whatever you need.

> Blessed [fortunate, prosperous, and favored by God] is the man who does not walk in the counsel of the wicked [following their advice and example], nor stand in the path of sinners, nor sit [down to rest] in the seat of scoffers (ridiculers).
>
> But his delight is in the law of the Lord, and on His law [His precepts and teachings] he [habitually] meditates day and night.
>
> And he will be like a tree *firmly planted [and fed] by streams of water,* which yields its fruit in its season; its leaf

does not wither; and in whatever he does, he prospers [and comes to maturity]. (Ps. 1:1–3 AMP)

My advice to you? Start speaking well of yourself and to yourself. Lay those leaves out flat every day to absorb the light of the Son. Photosynthesize. Transform. Convert CO_2 into oxygen. Take the negative and turn it into positive. Build rich soil with lots of nutrients your trunk can draw from. Tell yourself good things. Create a new you. Speak out loud, the way God did when He created the universe. Meditate on the Word throughout the day. Think about what you read. Chew on it, roll it around in your thoughts, and speak it out loud whenever you can. Build a layer of leaves that provides ongoing nutrients to your core that supports every facet of your life. This concept is so important I'm going to hit it from all sides, from top to bottom and all around, until you look up and say, "I get it! I see it now!"

By faith [that is, with an inherent trust and enduring confidence in the power, wisdom and goodness of God] we understand that the worlds (universe, ages) were framed and created [formed, put in order, and equipped for their intended purpose] by the word of God, so that what is seen was not made out of things which are visible. (Heb. 11:3 AMP)

It is by faith we understand that the whole world was made by God's command so

> what we see was made by something that cannot be seen. (Heb. 11:3 NCV)

If we look at these kinds of examples from nature and learn lessons from them, we can take our lives to a level we never knew existed. We'll find that $20 bill blowing around in the leaves—bills with all sorts of value.

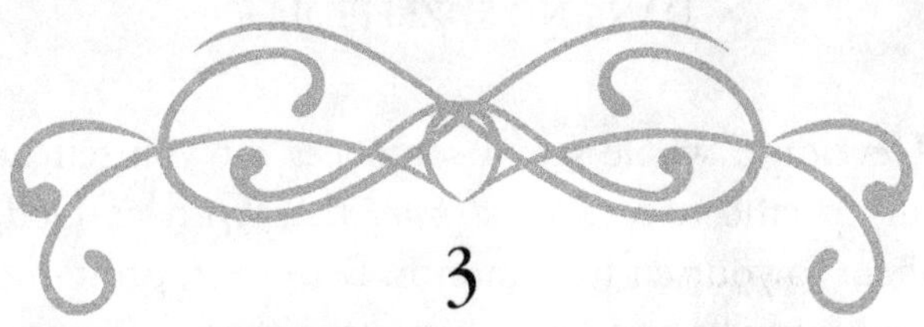

3
Words: Oodles of Leaves

A personal friend of ours, the late Dr. Paul Hegstrom of Life Skills International and author of numerous books, including *Grown up Children, Childhood Pain*, developed a course based on what I'm trying to expound upon. He contended that changing bad behavior starts with changing what you say about yourself. Week 1 of the Life Skills course begins with assigning a full page of good things to read to and about yourself. He assigned the same reading, every day, one sentence at a time. Repetition. It's how the brain was designed to grow and change, with pathways being firmly established. Your words really reflect who you are on the inside.

Develop a whole set of sentences for yourself catered to your specific needs, *based from* the Word of God, and read them to yourself for a month. Better yet, print out your favorite scriptures and keep them by you to read every day. Speak them out loud and see if you don't change from the inside out. Initially, you may not believe the things you read to yourself, but the system will begin to work, whether you believe it or not. It's a brain thing.

For example, if you say to yourself, "I am intelligent," believing it's true or not true is irrelevant. Your brain, hearing your voice saying that sentence, will eventually convince you that it's true. Your voice is the most convincing to your own mind. If someone else tells you you're smart, you'll just say, "Yeah, right." But when you tell yourself this, the subconscious sits up and takes notice. Like Jerry, you'll stop doubting every decision you make, because you come to believe you're intelligent and able to make a good decision. I say this again:

> For the word of God is alive and powerful. It is sharper than the sharpest two-edged sword, cutting between soul and spirit, between joint and marrow. It exposes our innermost thoughts and desires. (Heb. 4:12 NLT)

And so your spoken words are the same when you repeat them and believe them. This is the very thing that changes a caterpillar into a butterfly. As much as that is a physiological transformation, so is what I'm describing to you. And when you believe what God thinks about you…well, there's a great start to the day! Don't you know that God loves you for who you are? He made you, and He doesn't make mistakes. He's not a liar either. So when He says to the believer that you have the mind of Christ, the Son of the Living God, then you must be pretty intelligent.

> Spiritually alive, we have access to everything God's Spirit is doing, and can't be judged by unspiritual critics. Isaiah's question, "Is there anyone around who knows God's Spirit, anyone who knows what he is doing?" has been answered: Christ knows, and we have Christ's Spirit. (1 Cor. 2:15–16 MSG)
>
> But people who aren't spiritual can't receive these truths from God's Spirit. It all sounds foolish to them and they can't understand it, for only those who are spiritual can understand what the Spirit means. Those who are spiritual can evaluate all things, but they themselves cannot be evaluated by others.
>
> For, "Who can know the Lord's thoughts? Who knows enough to teach him?" But we understand these things, for we have the mind of Christ. (1 Cor. 2:14–16 NLT)

Epoxy is an extremely strong glue, but it takes two components mixed together to make it that way. One without the other doesn't work. It's when you mix the Word with the faith that develops as you read Scripture over and over that makes the Word you speak like epoxy. It will hold.

I have a skiing story to relay to you. My wife says this incident in our lives holds one of the most romantic things I've ever done. I don't know. I think I could easily top it, but I'll let her perception remain.

We went downhill-skiing at a resort with some friends. There were six of us. We were dropped off by the ski lift at the top of a hill. My wife saw that it was steeper than the others we had skied earlier in the day, and she determined in her mind that it was too much for her. She thought her skill level was not that of our friends, and so she said to us all, "I'm going to take my time down this one. You guys go ahead. I'll catch up." Fear had gripped her, I could tell. They all said, "Okay, so long," and shoved off. Someone must have skied past us right at that moment, because she said she counted five skiers go down the hill and assumed that I was one of them. In her thinking, she was alone in this unwelcome adventure.

She commenced going down the hill as slowly as possible, skiing all the way from one side of the steep hill to the other. The only thing is, it was so slow she was unable to "swish" her skis to make the turns. She ended up going straight into the waist-deep snow off the edge of the slope. As she was struggling to pull even one leg out, she said that a strong arm reached down and pulled her straight up out of the snow. That would be me. She was surprised and thankful in that split second of time, but when she looked up and saw that it was me, she cried with a combination of despair and joy. Her hero. Remember, she thought I had gone down with the rest of the group. She didn't know I was behind her the whole time, watching out for her. I swooshed in to her rescue seconds after the mishap.

Two points here: For one thing, if we really ever knew how much God loves us, I think it would completely change the way we live our lives. I know it would have changed the way she was skiing to know that I was behind her the whole time. God's got your back, always. That is, if He's the one you've put your trust in in life. He is always skiing behind us, sort of, making sure we make it. Of course He is. He loves us. Just because you can't sense God at times doesn't mean He isn't there working something out for you to succeed. Say this: "God's got my back. At all times, God's got me. I'm okay." Say it every morning, especially if you're facing something tough in your life. Mix some epoxy together and have confidence that it'll stick.

The second point has to do with what I instructed her to do next. Her trouble wasn't her technique, but more, it was the thinking approach she was using. She was too timid. I told her to ski like she was attacking that hill. I told her she had to view it like she was its master, not the other way around. I made her denounce out loud the fear she was feeling. God hates fear. It's a sin to engage in fear. Fear is a spirit, and it's not from Him. I had her repeat after me several times who she was (a child of the King) and had her proclaim a step-by-step plan of how she was going to handle this situation, which, for her, was daunting.

> For God did not give us a spirit of timidity (of cowardice, of craven and cringing and fawning fear), but [He has given us a spirit] of power and of love and of calm

> and well-balanced mind and discipline and self-control. (2 Tim. 1:7 AMPC)

She believed that scripture; she just needed to be reminded of it. Right then, she was like Peter stepping out of the boat to go to Jesus but getting distracted by the terrible storm at hand.

> And Peter answered him and said, Lord, if it be thou, bid me come unto thee on the water.
>
> And he said, Come. And when Peter was come down out of the ship, he walked on the water, to go to Jesus.
>
> But when he saw the wind boisterous, he was afraid; and beginning to sink, he cried, saying, Lord, save me.
>
> And immediately Jesus stretched forth his hand, and caught him, and said unto him, O thou of little faith, wherefore didst thou doubt? (Matt. 14:28–31 KJV)

As soon as she dropped a couple of familiar leaves onto her soil, I could see she was back to herself. She would not be taking her skis off and walking down the hill. No, no. You should have seen her swish, swish down that hill like a pro! I wish I had a before-and-after video. I could have used it as a "How to Ski Properly and What Not to Do" training piece. But the lesson is that if you really want something, you have to be aggressive, not passive. *You* do the directing in that which you fear. *You* change the course. *You* make it go the way you need it to go. You write your own ticket.

Of course, we all still laugh about the fear that I had to conquer that day. You see, there was one chair lift that was extremely high. My friends thought it was funny when they tricked me and I ended up on that lift again, asking, "This isn't that high one, is it?" It was my turn to talk to myself and get the apprehension out.

Not to beat a dead horse (what a terrible saying), but I can't express enough how important your spoken words are. What a lightning bolt of revelation when you come to really understand this and utilize the principle. This is the single most effective concept Dr. Hegstrom found so productive in people changing their own lives. I know, because I asked him what he thought the greatest tool in the toolbox was. He found great results even with inmates in prison. Check it out.

Repetition of saying good things to yourself works in the subconscious. It reprograms and rewires the brain to believe a different system than what it's always known.

How did you learn how to tie your shoe as a five-year-old? Repetition, right? You just kept trying and trying. This step following that step fell right into place the more you did it. It got easier and easier. Now you can carry on a conversation while you bend down and tie away and not even think about it. It's a brain thing. When the brain develops a well-worn pathway, it protects that pathway with a coating called a myelin sheath. With repeated use, the brain knows you're trying to make it the go-to pathway. Learn to work *with* your brain and make the pathways strong that *you* choose.

Why does thinking burn calories? Because there's actual electrical energy going on when you make a choice. Read one of the recommended books on the brain from the

"Recommended Reading" at the back of the book, and you'll learn why we do the things we do and how to work with your own brain. There's a reason you choose to sit in the same seat when you enter the classroom, and on and on.

There are so many things we just never knew before about brain function. Studies are now discovering them. Did you know, for example, that exercising faith is the number 1 best exercise for the brain? That's according to an agnostic author and his self-proclaimed atheist coauthor.[1] These physiological principles have always been there, and they've always worked. It's how God created us.

You'll find it hard to say to yourself, "Oh, I'm such a fool—where did I put my keys?" when you've been saying, "I am valuable. I have the mind of Christ. I'm strong in the Lord and in the power of His might. I'm more than able to do everything I need to do. God loves me."

You'll start to catch yourself regarding what comes out of your mouth. Phrases you used to repeat, like, "That just kills me," "He drives me crazy," or "I'll probably die young like the rest of the men in my family," will start to "grate on your last nerve." You'll connect with the system and get proficient at it, changing your whole manner of speech. Remember Jerry from chapter 2? He made a simple adjustment that changed his world, and his future.

But this can work in the negative just as easily. How do people become obsessive, opinionated, racist, fearful, phobia-dominated, or even insane? Couldn't it be the brainwashing they themselves have allowed? Double-check yourself against what God has said about you in the Word. He's your manufacturer, after all. Maybe you should follow His advice.

What have you rehearsed over and over in your heart? The leaves on your forest floor can be filled with thoughts, words, and beliefs that have dropped over the years and are now feeding your tree with poison: bitterness, anger, hatred, unforgiveness, and the like. You may have been told something as a child and you have believed it to be the truth. Always remember that what you feed on is what you come to believe as true.

I have had people say to me that some character traits or personality flaws cannot be changed. They say, "You're born that way, and that's all there is to it." And yet I've heard testimony after testimony of those who have done it. They've overcome. They've changed for *life* whatever they considered to be a flaw for them. They're different from the inside out, and everyone who knew them can see it.

Here's a couple of great applications to this principle. See if you don't notice a difference shortly after implementing it. Do you feel you have fallen out of love with your spouse? Try forcibly "changing your mind" by saying out loud every day to yourself how much you love him/her, even though you might not feel that way. Every day, in your imagination, review the things that first attracted you to them. If it doesn't fix the problem, it will certainly help. Or try the principle with forgiveness toward someone. You don't have to feel the emotion for the principle to begin to take effect; you just have to say it out loud. Eventually, the feeling will come. The disdain will leave. You won't cringe anymore at the mention of that person's name.

Save yourself from yourself. Declare and decree the thing into existence. Find yourself swish-swishing in life instead of being off to the side, missing all the fun. It's a major part of your salvation package to use words and expect results.

4 Blooming with Real Purpose

Anybody who knows me knows my heart goes pitter-pat when I see flowers. I'll make a U-turn in the car to go back and "smell the roses" if I see a place of interest. Although they are beautiful (and that's the part I love), my spiritual observance is that they sure know how to do it right! And again as I observe nature to see what God has set in place, I ask, "How can I model that perfection in my own life? How can I bloom?" It's one thing to do it; it's another to do it *right*.

When I was thirty, we had a neighbor and friend who was eighty years old named Olga. She maintained a garden that was out of this world. Those who drove by would enjoy the fruits of her labor because her talent spilled over to the bank on the opposite side of the road. She would plant a few phlox across the way each year in all their varied color. Year after year, those flowers would spread out until the entire side of the road was splashed with pink, lavender, white, blue, and purple. Driving along that stretch of road was an experience like Dorothy and her friends had skipping through the field of poppies in *The Wizard of Oz*. Olga had poppies, too, by the way, and they were tall and brilliant. By midsummer, she could have charged admission to go into her backyard.

But Olga had a secret to her garden's glory. She lived in a small house nestled in between competing forests. Those forests allowed a myriad of leaves to drop onto her yard, and she would harvest them every autumn. Five-foot-tall Olga would gather them up and, with her spade, dig holes around her perennials all over the garden and "plant" those leaves. She had the richest soil in the county. And her magnificent flowers would breathe out their thanks to her in all their splendor. They weren't eating grilled cheese; they were eating hearty steak, potatoes, and asparagus at every meal.

The relationship between the soil and a tree (or plant) is inseparable. The leaves produce the tree's food in the growing season, then give nutrients back to the roots at a later time. Nutrients are released in decomposition. It's almost like the salmon swimming upstream to give its life for future generations.

Here's the thing: Those flowers were somewhat indiscriminate. They took what they needed from the soil, from what was available. And what they were drawing from in Olga's garden was most obviously causing them to flourish. But plants sometimes take in what kills them. We, too, can take in that which poisons us. Leaves (words) from other trees (people) land on our soil (heart), and it's *our choice* to receive them or reject them. You can allow them to grow you or to kill you.

> I call heaven and earth to witness against you that today I have set before you life or death, blessing or curse. Oh, that you would choose life; that you and your children might live! (Deut. 30:19 NLT)

Just because someone throws a pop bottle onto your leaf pile doesn't mean you need to try to digest it. Here's the next level, if you can handle it.

I purposely stay away from people who are not good for me. Their spoken leaves aren't good for my forward progress.

Jesus did this as well, many times and in many forms. How rude, one might say, but it was Jesus who did it nonetheless. Check out this lesson:

> But when Jesus heard it, He answered him saying, Fear not: believe only, and she shall be made whole.
>
> And when He came into the house, *He suffered no man to go in*, save Peter, and James and John, and the father and the mother of the maiden. And all wept, and bewailed her; but He said, Weep not; she is not dead, but sleepeth. And they laughed Him to scorn, knowing that she was dead.
>
> And *He put them all out*, and took her by the hand, and called, saying, Maid arise.

> And her spirit came again, and she arose straightway: and He commanded to give her meat. (Luke 8:50–55 KJV)

First of all, Peter, James, and John were the three He consistently took with Him. Why? Perhaps they were the ones most tuned in to His purpose? Perhaps they were the ones who spoke right words?

Second, in this scripture passage, Jesus didn't want to hear *it* from the people. He had a mission to accomplish. The weeping and wailing in his ears and the words, or rather the facts, he was told, like, "She's dead. You're too late. Don't bother," would not help accomplish what was needed.

Can't you just see him ushering them out the door or, more likely, instructing bold Peter to do so? Again, in our politically correct world, this was a rude action to take. But there was only room for one of two choices: faith speakers or doubt speakers, life choosers or accepters of death. Otherwise, you take the risk of becoming double-minded. You risk the fact that you may actually consider what's being said! Taking this action can be compared to what farmers call planting mingled seed. It's when there is weed seed mixed in with crop seed. How do you harvest a good crop of hay when there is yellow rocket or dandelion all over the field?

Faith is the only choice that pleases the Father. A number of scriptures detail that fact. If you're not in faith, you're in doubt, and you better get rid of doubt in every form in which it comes.

> But without faith it's impossible to please Him. (Heb. 11:6 KJV)

> For whatsoever is not of faith is sin. (Rom. 14:23b KJV)
>
> When Jesus heard it, he marveled, and said to them that followed, Verily I say unto you, I have not found so great faith, no, not in Israel. (Matt. 8:10 KJV)
>
> Be it unto you according to your faith. (Matt. 9:29 KJV)

Jesus was quite blatant in his approach to choosing life, and he identified those who were choosing death with unconcealed, deliberate candor. He attempted to snap them into reality (the Father's brand of reality) and to cause them to begin to live life the only way to victory. He identified them as "brood of snakes" (Matt. 3:7, 12:34, 23:33) and "white-washed tombs" (Matt. 23:27). Jesus was no wimp and afraid of no man.

Blooming does not come about by accident. Getting some types of flowers to bloom, like poinsettias, requires a whole lot of detailed instructions to be followed, having to do with timing, lighting, temperature, etc. It's Christ in us causing us to bloom. But blooming has to be pursued, and that, on purpose.

We only have so much time in life. Stress can squelch blooming, both in plants and in people. Anything that disrupts or detours you should be cast aside. Timing is everything with God, so stay alert. If Satan can delay you from the appointed time, he may be able to foil the whole deal at hand.

Here's the point: You may not need to call people out or call them names, but you will have to keep certain folks at arm's length in your life. The method may differ, but the end result has got to keep you on track. Decipher people in your life. To *decipher* means to untangle, interpret, unencrypt, or translate. It doesn't mean these people are bad; it just means they don't fit in your life right now.

The "Why" Behind the "You"

This deciphering principle was reaffirmed in me from reading a biography about George Washington Carver. He abided by this same rule. He was one focused fellow!

Knowing God and what seed God had planted inside him, at some point, G. W. Carver gathered the boldness to shun certain people who he knew were not going to contribute to his purpose. He wouldn't meet or converse with them after they had traveled many miles for that exact purpose. That's knowing who you are in Christ! What an example of Jesus's use of deciphering and discernment. And yet "What a rude action to take!" would be the view of most who don't use God's brand of discernment. If Carver could be bold, knowing who it was that stood behind him, maybe we should restrict who we allow admittance into our world. You can't eat everything off the menu, anyway. So choose carefully.

Carver also had God's brand of persistence. His resolution and tenacity, in his particular gifting, were something to be admired.

In January of 1921, he was invited to speak in front of the members of Congress, and yet he was not allowed to enter up the front steps of the building. He attempted to honor the invitation to speak, and yet he met the obstacle of the doorman who kicked his suitcase aside. It was God alone who watched over him that day and over what He had placed inside Mr. Carver to advance humanity.

> Moreover whom he did predestinate, them he also called: and whom he called, them he also justified: and whom he justified, them he also glorified.
>
> What shall we then say to these things? *If God be for us, who can be against us?* (Rom. 8:30–31 KJV)

As Carver began his presentation, members of Congress laughed at him. But he continued. They soon recognized his genius and anointing from God. They quieted down, and subsequently, each one gave up their own allotted speaking time in order to allow him more time to complete his presentation.[2] Look it up in history. It happened. What an outcome for the day, ordained and planned by God.

Once you know the *why* behind the *you*, you will scrutinize everything in your life. I can tell you that the why is not just to have a job, just to make money, just to pay taxes, just to own a home, or just to have a family. Yes, God is interested in keeping you supplied and caring for you, but that's not the whole of your life. The question remains, The one who made you, the architect of your life, and the one who's put purpose in you is the one you have to pursue to discover the why behind the you. He's the potter; you're the clay. Are you a cup or a plate? Who are you? Find out from Him. And then don't allow distractions to take you away from that purpose.

When you know the why behind the you and begin to move in that direction, all of God's favor comes in to assist you. Why? Because you're now living life in the zone. For Carver, he had boldness and ability to *not take in* the poisons he saw and heard that day—the jeers, the laughter, and the comments. G. W. Carver was focused, and nothing could distract him. He knew this opportunity of demonstrating his profound discoveries, in those single moments of faith, would make great strides for not only the country but also his students back home. So he cast out the fear and degradation and moved forward.

I often think of these events and others that are documented in George Washington Carver's lifetime. He exemplified everything I'm trying to express here. He is one man I would like to meet and talk to in heaven, if he will agree to meet with me. (That is written in jest.)

He replicated himself in young men by teaching them what he knew.

Have you ever seen a plant with suckers growing by the main stem? We had a birch tree that didn't fare well one winter. We received a heavy late snow after it had already sent up its sap to produce buds. It took nearly a week for the snow to melt away, and in that time, the tree died. In response, its safety mechanism kicked in. It produced some thirty little saplings coming up through the soil from the strong root system.

That was exactly what Carver did. He had a strong root system connected to God, and he used it to produce many strong, godly scientists like him.

One of the young boys he mentored, Henry Wallace, later became vice president of the United States under Franklin D. Roosevelt. From all that Carver had poured into him, it only made sense that Wallace serve as secretary to the

US Department of Agriculture. The leaves Carver dropped onto little Henry's soil have benefitted us all, generations later.

We affect others in ways we sometimes don't realize. Olga's eighty-year-old wisdom profoundly influenced my thirty-year-old wife. I am thankful to her for that.

George was not a special person any more than you or I, yet one of the principles that set him apart was his ability to keep his divine focus. You and I can attain the same, if only we would. He fulfilled his destiny. If you read of his methodology, you'll find he definitely operated in the zone! Reading his biography has influenced me to stretch further to hear God's voice.

The more you feed on the Son's Words and get them into your spirit-man, the more that is what will come out of your mouth. It will become not what you believe, or just what you say, but who you are. Jesus replicates and recreates Himself in us. Like Him, you will come to act in what everyone calls the supernatural. This is living life in the zone. You can become a flower that keeps on blooming and creates a special, unique, particular beauty for all to see and take advantage of.

5

Growing Up to Bloom: Exchanging Positive for Negative

It's the subtle or veiled words from friends and loved ones that can harm and misdirect you the most. This chapter holds the basics of my childhood story that helped form my personality and method of operation in life.

It's difficult to filter through everything that is said to you in your life, but it's a practice that *must* be diligently observed in order for you to flourish and bloom. You must decipher words spoken over you. It is crucial. Words hurt, to be sure, but when you give them heed, they can also afflict your purpose. Hang around those who appreciate you for who you are, around those who use their mouthpiece for sweet, not bitter.

> And so blessing and cursing come pouring out of the same mouth. Surely, my brothers and sisters, this is not right! Does a spring of water bubble out with both fresh water and bitter water? Does a fig tree produce olives, or a grapevine produce figs? No, and you can't draw fresh water from a salty spring. (James 3:10–12 NLT)

This was troublesome for me as a kid. I had a bit of a rugged upbringing in some ways. Kids can be cruel, and all boys have to deal with that at some level. Girls can be cruel too, I guess. I dealt with the cruelty by fighting. What did I fight over the most? It seemed their word choices set me off, if you know what I mean. Name-calling is a trigger for most people, is it not?

I fought all the time until I acquired the reputation as the class fighter. My classmates came to get me to fight *their* battles too. That got me into trouble. My second-grade teacher wrote, "Dan's a leader. We just have to get him leading in the right direction." So I was held back a year. That'll bring out some anger in a kid. My teachers at the school my parents moved me to next only exacerbated the problem.

Don't we all have something? Don't we all have certain things in our lives that could be more than just memories, if we let them?

So I started collecting bullets. I didn't even know that different guns took different shells, but it was a result of the inner rage growing inside. Ah, to have known then what I know now! I have insight into what America is experiencing today with angry youth, since I was one. I wish someone had pressed in, past the anger and rebellion, to listen to me when I was young. If only they had taught me how to deal with my frustrations.

Nothing ever came of the bullet collection, but I can tell you that the roughness I experienced helped shape me. For others, it may have weakened or crushed their resolve in life, but for me it only intensified it. It made me strong. It made me an overcomer. My dad gave up on spankings because I refused to cry. So they kept me in for a week as punishment. For me, that hurt more.

I'd always had a lot of confidence, although it was placed in myself and not in God. I grew accustomed to employing that well-worn pathway in my brain of "I win. No matter what, I win."

As a building contractor, I remember once setting up lights and working through the night shingling a roof for a business because it was going to rain. I won, even against the rain.

When Suzi and I were first married, her new dog ran away and didn't know where home was. I found him against all odds, after he had gone missing for two weeks. Now, those were stories of faith for another book, but I won, even against a lost dog.

I remember in football, Coach placed me as a guard against players who were far greater in height and weight than I. He kept me in that position because, you guessed it, I won, even against guys bigger than I.

I remember these events because they reaffirm in my soul that I am a winner in life. That may sound bold to some, but it's scriptural. In Jesus, we always get the victory. We are the winners.

> But thanks be to God, which giveth us the victory through our Lord Jesus Christ. (1 Cor. 15:7 KJV)

Throughout my youth, I learned that pain could be a blessing, because when everyone quit, I could win if I could endure. Someone once said, "Pain is just weakness leaving." As a youth, sweat was not an issue with me. Exhaustion was not an issue. Getting dirty was not an issue. Injuries were not an issue. At the point where guys were throwing up from running one hundred one-hundred-yard sprints in football practice, I learned to endure hardship. I endured it for that *win* on Friday night, and because of this, "you cannot break my spirit." That came from the harshness I endured both at home and in grade school. There's an expression common to those teaching children that was true in my case: I *caught* more than I was *taught*. I had to learn how to survive and how to make it through anything life could throw in my direction.

Maybe entering Christianity, I had a "leg up" on some people because of my personality and what I went through as a youngster. I was, and am, a tough contender. I was tough against others in sports. Now, I'm tough against the devil. The following scripture wasn't hard for me to put in my back pocket and carry around with me. I understood the principle of standing my ground against an enemy.

> For we are not fighting against flesh-and-blood enemies, but against evil rulers and authorities of the unseen world, against mighty powers in this dark world, and against evil spirits in the heavenly places. Therefore, put on every piece of God's armor so you will be able to resist the enemy in the time of evil. Then after the battle you will still be standing firm. Stand your ground, putting on the belt of truth and the body armor of God's righteousness. (Eph. 6:12–14 NLT)

As a kid, I felt as though I was a flower trying to push through a crack in the concrete rather than growing up in a nicely tended flowerbed.

It wasn't until I was around twenty and a Christian for a few years that I started the process of backing off my audacity and allowing God to take over. I gradually transferred my self-confidence to confidence through and from Him.

In high school, I excelled in sports and had a lot of friends, including girls. Football and wrestling allowed me to "vent" in acceptable forms, but I was an angry fellow inside. Life was not fair in my young view, and I was going to take all I could get. I learned a system, and it wasn't a good one. This was my creed: do whatever you need to do, but don't get caught. I truly believe that had not drastic changes been made (and I was moved away from home) like so many around me, I would have been in some deep trouble.

In my teens, if I did what was acceptable in a grown-up's view, I got a pat on the back and was left alone. Then I could devise my get-ahead schemes. I'm not proud of some of those schemes, but God saw me, loved me through it, and rescued me.

Not always was it anger that motivated me. From a young age, I was taught how to work. From simple household chores to waxing and buffing the basement floor, I found that work got me valuable kudos and time off. For example, I was fourteen years old, and I knew my dad wanted the house painted. So I got money from him in order to buy the best paint, which was what I knew he would buy, and I painted on *my* schedule. If he drove in the driveway and saw progress, he would leave me alone. I could hop on my bike and the summer was mine. I played baseball with my friends whenever I wanted, as long as I got the house painted.

That understanding was never voiced, either by my dad or myself, but it was the system in place. In the negative, it's called manipulation. That was how I viewed it at that time. I was manipulating the situation. But on the positive side (and God always has one), I became a self-motivator because of the rewards I experienced. My dad appreciated that I was a hard worker. Rarely did I get the "Go dig one hundred dandelions" punishment, because I kept the lawn mowed before a complaint could be raised. Our house and lawn always looked nice. My dad might never have thrown a ball to me or gone to my wrestling match or football game, as he deemed those events a waste of time, but he certainly taught me how to work. In later years, I had to bring work into balance.

But here's where the hard work principle brought me: In my early twenties, I was in college, attempting to get a degree in agribusiness. Although I never pursued a career in that direction, during that time I worked as a hired man on a big dairy farm. That farm corporation was a successful grade-A milk producer, but the interior of the milk house didn't reflect that fact. It was a sight to see. As required, they kept the stainless steel bulk tank shiny silver, but everything else was speckled brown from flies. The clear pipeline was no longer clear. The flies had so covered it that I thought it was rusty metal. It took pulling a couple of all-nighters, but I cleaned the interior of the milk house to a spit-shine appearance. Then I painted it on my own time. What a difference it made! And what a difference it made with the family who ran the business. Of all the hired milkers they'd had up to that point, I had shown the most initiative.

I strove to be that way at all my places of employment. I always did my best and over and above, wherever possible. It not only guaranteed my job when others might have taken it, but it usually also resulted in advancement. I had more than one employer want me to stay when I gave my notice.

Here was my thinking on all the jobs where I worked. It might be easiest to demonstrate using the example of the dairy farm: all the plowing, all the manure spreading, all the planting, all the hay mowing, all the corn harvesting, all the feeding, all the milking, all the veterinary care, and all the special cow breeding culminated in the white liquid pumped into that little room with the shiny bulk tank, waiting for pickup.

If this was the best milk money could buy, how could its holding place be so unfitting? A business owner does all he can to put out that product that everyone wants, and sometimes it's the littlest thing that wrecks the finest results.

> Take us the foxes, the little foxes, that spoil the vines: for our vines have tender grapes. (Song of Sol. 2:15 KJV)

So it is in our lives. Sometimes it's as small as a few wrong words we've accepted as truth, like I did as a kid growing up. Remember, it was the words, the little words, the name-calling, which caused the fighting, that got me into trouble.

I still visit them there at the farm. I'm a lifelong friend. They poured into my life and taught me things as much as I tried to add value to their business. Their leaves fell on my soil. I watched them and came to appreciate the hard work I'd been taught as a kid. I learned organization, structure, goal-setting, focus, and working toward that all-important end product: fruit fit for harvest. Much of this book wouldn't have the growing principles I've observed in life if I didn't have the farm experience. Further, Suzi and I not only did make wedding plans but also lifelong goals as she sat on the fender of the tractor while I raked drying hay the summer of our marriage.

So many of Jesus's parables revolve around nature, people's work habits, their motivations, and what we are involved in from day to day. We bring our own personality into our Christian walk. The observations I've made about plant growth started from watching the stages of corn growth in the field. I received message after message from God about life from the farming I participated in. God is the best farmer. After all, He planted Jesus and harvested us. It's our job to figure out how to bloom for Him.

> For we are his workmanship, created in Christ Jesus unto good works, which God hath before ordained that we should walk in them. (Eph. 2:10 KJV)

6

A Little Help from Leaves Dropped by Other Trees

Everyone needs to be validated to some extent. But when it comes to your potential, you must draw from God, not from others—unless you see that their wisdom (fruit) is valuable to pick for your own personal growth.

I've built over a dozen authentic log houses in my life, for myself, for others, and with others. Log homes were my dream and my passion as a twenty-two-year-old young man. Ask my wife. In college, she caught me skipping class one fine, sunny afternoon. I was lying on the newly mown grass in the center of campus, taking in the fragrance of spring. On my textbook, I was building a log house out of toothpicks that I had taken from the student center. As she walked by on the sidewalk, she asked, "Don't you have class?" I countered with a simple, "Yep." My heart wasn't in class; it was in finding logs to use for our house.

God found me my giant toothpicks. I took down the logs for my first house from an old barn on my lunch breaks and after work, milking cows. But the real story worth telling is in how I acquired those logs.

I had driven past a farm with an old log barn that was falling down. As usual, I heard that voice deep inside. It said, "I'll help you build a house from those logs." I backed up and pulled in the driveway. I knocked on the farmhouse door, and within minutes, the logs were mine. They were given to me by an eighty-year-old German farmer named Wilbur Seifert. I'll never forget the man. He saw something in me worth valuing; that got my attention. He's long gone now, but his influence over my life is far-reaching.

We shook hands on it, back when a handshake and a man's word meant something. He taught me, by example, to be a person of integrity *first.* How? About a week after our agreement, he was offered $2,000 for those same logs. He refused, declaring that he had given them to a young couple wanting to use them to build a house.

That was a lot of money to me back then. It was hard for my brain to register that he turned it down. Two weeks later, the potential buyer upped his offer to $5,000! Still, Wilbur declined. Even when the man, who happened to be a lawyer, stated that he could easily get him out of his verbal agreement with me, Wilbur held to his promise. That impressed me tremendously, and now I saw something extra worth valuing in Mr. Seifert. I saw a man who stuck by his word.

> Who may worship in your sanctuary, Lord?… Those who despise flagrant sinners, and honor the faithful followers of the Lord, and keep their promises even when it hurts. (Ps. 15:1, 4 NLT)
>
> He keeps his word even to his own disadvantage and does not change it [for his own benefit]. (Ps. 15:4b AMP)

When I was growing up, my nickname among family members was Slipshod Dan. I learned all the shortcuts to get what I wanted. Oh, I took out the garbage, when asked—no problem. The issue was that I didn't return the garbage can back to the kitchen, because my bike was there, tempting me to hop on and ride away. And anyway, they didn't ask me to bring it back; they only asked me to take it out. My integrity as a kid was a little on the low side, to say the least. How the Word of God has changed me!

I've told the story of Wilbur Seifert many times in my life. Every time, it reminds me of who I'm supposed to be. I enjoyed our talks, as at times he would visit with me as I worked and told me stories of his life. I learned his message well, not to mention the scripture in the previous box that it illustrates.

To my own hurt, just like Wilbur, I have lost out numerous times in my life in order to keep my word. However, I've never felt short-changed. The opportunity to see who I've grown into in those times is reward enough. God has always abundantly supplied for me, as you'll read in later chapters. Honor His Word, allow it to change you, and He will honor His covenant with you. I do my best to follow through, because God always follows through with His Word to me.

> I will confirm my covenant with you and your descendants after you, from generation to generation. This is the everlasting covenant: I will always be your God and the God of your descendants after you. (Gen. 17:7 NLT)

Wilbur Seifert contributed to my life, as have others. Here's the principle from nature that I have observed: There's not a fence around a tree in the woods that says, "My leaves just feed me." We are interdependent. In fact, we're made for interdependence, not independence. We're made for connection. You will not have enough time in your life to figure it out all on your own and pay for all the mistakes you'll make. Take advantage of those who have gone before you. Glean from them what you can.

I Know You're Growing, But What Are You Growing Into?

The leaves dropped by other trees around you can be used for nutrition, true, but everything must be broken down and looked at—evaluated, if you will. And then only the parts needed should be taken in. Tune out the rest. Ignore it. You must push your whole self into life if you're going to grow strong and tall and produce fruit. It'll take hard work. It's more like building a watch than building a wall. You can't make a mistake here.

The earth is in itself a filtering process for water. Sometimes it can be okay to drink water straight out of an artesian well, for example. But if you want the purest water, you have to analyze every microbe and impurity that might be in that water.

Imagine your life as that water. After you have received everything your parents, teachers, siblings, and friends have said to you, you have to do the final examination and look at what you are believing and saying to yourself from their influence. This is one of the hardest things to do, because sometimes you've been drinking these words for so long they seem to taste just fine. The bitter has become acceptable, palatable. But if it's not what God says about you, it can't be taken in. By the time you've thought something twice, you've already started to form a pathway in the brain.

> "Watch out!" Jesus warned them. "Beware of the yeast of the Pharisees and Sadducees."

> Then at last they understood that he wasn't speaking about the yeast in bread, but about the deceptive teaching of the Pharisees and Sadducees. (Matt. 16:6, 12 NLT)

One of the greatest things God gave us is the power of choice. One of the most detrimental things God gave us is the power of choice. That's not a typo. Handled correctly, it's wonderful for us to be able to choose for ourselves. And in God's view, He loves it when we choose to trust His ways over the crowd's ways.

The truth is, everything is speaking to you. When you sit down to eat, everything at the table speaks to you. "Is the plate clean? Should I eat this? Can I trust the cook? Will this give me indigestion?" There's so much to filter through. Every step you take, your sight, smell, touch, and hearing absorb all that surrounds you. Via the senses, your subconscious is constantly taking everything in.

Don't forget, Eve was tempted by what she *saw*. She saw that the fruit was good and forgot all about what God had said. She *trusted* what she saw and regarded it more than what God's command was concerning it.

> And when the woman saw that the tree was good for food, and that it was pleasant to the eyes, and a tree to be desired to make one wise, she took of the fruit thereof, and did eat, and gave also unto her husband with her; and he did eat. (Gen. 3:6 KJV)

Be careful what you give heed to.

For example, you drive along and the day speaks to you, saying, "Oh, it's a beautiful day!" It happens so fast it's automatic. And then this happens: you see a dead dog on the side of the road and it speaks to you, saying, "That's so sad!" Do you ponder it and allow it to take you to depression? Do you meander down Despair Street until it causes you to say, "What's the use? We're all going to die anyway!"? For many years in her young life, my wife focused on the negative, and it took her to depression. Using the principle of refocusing her attention every day, she was able to pull herself out of its grip.

You must filter everything. Everywhere you go, you've got to ask the right questions. Is this good for me? Is there something here for me to learn? Will this add to my life and to my potential, or will it detour me? I liked what I saw and heard from Wilbur Seifert, so I took it in.

It takes a concerted effort to direct your thoughts—and practice! As you're driving along, don't allow your thoughts to lope along. Don't let them roam and stray from the intent of your mind's purpose. Reel them in. You're actually building your own mental fences.

If we compare your mind to an orchestra, you are the conductor of all the instruments that are playing. You tell the drums to beat softer. You bring in the flutes, and don't forget the little triangle at just the right moment. But you have to make sure your instruments are in tune and playing in harmony with one another. Now you've got the symphony of life, and you're headed for the zone.

For the rest, brethren, whatever is true, whatever is worthy of reverence and is

> honorable and seemly, whatever is just, whatever is pure, whatever is lovely and lovable, whatever is kind and winsome and gracious, if there is any virtue and excellence, if there is anything worthy of praise, think on and weigh and take account of these things [fix your minds on them]. (Phil. 4:8 AMPC)

Only think on those things that are positive. That's a commandment, written in commandment form. And consider this scripture:

> Pleasant words are as a honeycomb, sweet to the mind and healing to the body. (Prov. 16:24 AMPC)

Let God take care of the crud in your life. Ask Him to, and He will. Then, because the Word of God is like a great hunting dog that goes about and does the work for you, you can concentrate on your purpose in life. As you learn it, the Word will flush out wrong thoughts, identifying those that need to go. The front paw on that dog will come up, and the tail will go straight and stiff. Then the stare, my goodness, the stare! You won't be able to get away from it. The Word will point at what's erroneous and what you need to fix. It will fetch and bring you thoughts you need to keep.

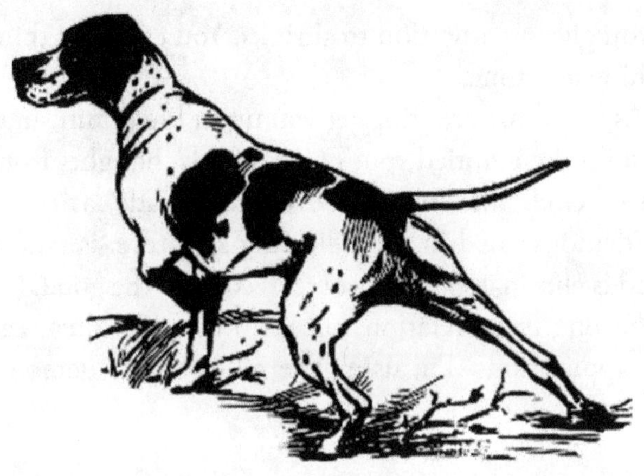

I love the following scripture. It's the Word, and the Word only, that can fix us up and orchestrate our lives.

> All Scripture is inspired by God and is useful to teach us what is true and to make us realize what is wrong in our lives. It corrects us when we are wrong and teaches us to do what is right. God uses it to prepare and equip his people to do every good work. (2 Tim. 3:16–17 NLT)

It's great to be a self-corrector, utilizing truths from God's Word as your mold and repair manual. Then you can stay focused on what God's put you on the planet to accomplish. And you can trust Him to pave the way for you. Stay focused. Stay in the middle of the road; don't land yourself in the ditch on either side. Whatever you focus on grows; whatever you give no attention to shrinks. You can only think on one thing at a time.

As areas that are tripping you up in life diminish, make sure to fill the emptied spot of crud with thoughts from the Word of God. The mistake commonly made, as comparatively demonstrated in the following scripture, is that when the bad is eliminated, it is not replaced with the good. (There may be one interpretation for Scripture, but there can be many applications. I'm using the following to demonstrate a principle.)

> When the unclean spirit is gone out of a man, he walketh through dry places, seeking rest; and finding none, he saith, I will return unto my house whence I came out.
>
> And when he cometh, he findeth it swept and garnished. Then goeth he, and taketh to him seven other spirits more wicked than himself; and they enter in, and dwell there: and the last state of that man is worse than the first. (Luke 11:24–26 KJV)

As a twenty-three-year-old with the rest of my life ahead of me, I knew I had to change. I knew Wilbur Seifert did what was right in turning down money in order to follow through with what he had spoken to me. It was right for his character, and it was right according to the Word of God. I changed my thinking and lined it up with that principle.

I sleep very well at night, holding principles like these. My brain can relax and be at peace, so to speak. The brain is an amazing, changeable, fixable, adaptable, trainable piece of equipment that God has given to us. Use it to its fullest potential. Don't squander its abilities, or your life.

> I love the Lord, because he hath heard my voice and my supplications. Because he hath inclined his ear unto me, therefore will I call upon him as long as I live. (Ps. 16:1–2 KJV)

7

Salvation: Tapped into the Vine and Getting Connected

I remember when my wife and I were married for only a couple of years. We belonged to a church, and at one point I said to her, "I'm not sure if, when the storms of life come, this church is feeding us the principles that will get us through." I remember discussion after discussion with her about the full scope of the word *salvation* and it's conceptual use in such scriptures as this:

> That if thou shalt confess with thy mouth the Lord Jesus, and shalt believe in thine heart that God hath raised him from the dead, thou shalt be saved.
>
> For with the heart man believeth unto righteousness; and with the mouth confession is made unto salvation. (Rom. 10:9–10 KJV)

(There it is again: "With the mouth *confession* is made.") As a new believer, she contended that salvation strictly applied to the salvation that sends you to heaven when you die. I tried to convey to her that it included that and so much more. Salvation includes your everyday life and applying every piece of godly wisdom you can implement. It's not a single word with a single definition, but more like a package.

Salvation starts with believing and then confessing with your mouth, as the scripture says, but the full scope of the Bible word *Sozos* (Greek word used in the Bible for *salvation*) takes you to the zone. It continues to save you and fill you and bless you and inform you and complete you and grow you and heal you and prosper you and change you and expand you and protect you and reproduce you into others, because you just can't keep quiet about it all! It gives you joy and peace in your life. The word includes *rescue* and *escape* but also includes *freedom*. The reality is, it's life as God has it and as He desires for you. Abundant life, He terms it.

> The thief does not come except to steal, and to kill, and to destroy. I have come that they may have life, and that they may have it more abundantly. (John 10:10 NKJV)

Abundant life. How else could someone who's been beaten time and again, left for dead, and so much more be happy to be about the work of the kingdom? How could he be so happy about his salvation? I'm speaking of the apostle Paul. Just listen to the following scripture:

> They were severely beaten and then they were thrown into prison. The jailer was ordered to make sure they didn't escape.

> So the jailer put them into the inner dungeon and clamped their feet in the stocks.
>
> Around midnight Paul and Silas were praying and singing hymns to God, and the other prisoners were listening. Suddenly, there was a massive earthquake, and the prison was shaken to its foundations. All the doors immediately flew open, and the chains of every prisoner fell off! (Acts 16:23–26 NLT)

With them held in stocks in the darkest, dankest, most disease-ridden of dungeons, I'm supposing they didn't allow Paul and Silas out of the stocks for bathroom breaks, if you get the picture. And yet through all the pain, stench, and despair, they used the one resource that was left unchained. They used their mouths to speak and sing praises to God, ultimately changing the ending of their story. It was not one of death and gloom. God did not leave them to rot in prison. He loved those men, yes, but I believe what He responded to was their faith-filled words. He has to! He set up the system, and those who honor it will get His attention. Of course, the entire New Testament church heard of their persecution and was pressing into God's system of words on their behalf to change the circumstances. They were praying.

It's a spiritual law that was enacted. Paul and Silas were in the zone that night. They were speaking the right words, moving in the faith realm. And things happened. Things didn't happen because Paul and Silas were special; God works on behalf of anyone who believes in Him and uses words the way He created them to work. Whether Abraham, David, or the apostle Paul, these are people who defied the negative situations they found themselves in. They used faith-filled words like God did when He created the world and every living thing in it.

Keep your hope in God. It's more powerful than you can ever imagine.

> Lead me by your truth and teach me, for you are the God who saves me. All day long I put my hope in you. (Ps. 25:5 NLT)
>
> The Lord directs the steps of the godly. He delights in every detail of their lives. Though they stumble, they will never fall, for the Lord holds them by the hand. (Ps. 37:23–24 NLT)

Tapped into the Vine

Paul and Silas were inexplicably tapped into the vine. It was their driving force to please the Father. Their salvation rescued them that day. When you're tapped into the vine, you get all the nutritive juices from that vine. Love begets love. Jesus loves us first, then that love causes us to respond back with love.

In horticulture class, my wife learned how to graft plants. She made slits in the branch and in the tree and stuck them together, interweaving those slits. Then she wrapped the "damaged" branch with tape until the graft took over. The cutoff branch now received all its life-giving fluids, minerals, and sustenance from that tree. Have you ever seen an apple tree with each branch containing a different kind of apple? Grafting. It's amazing. The branch maintains its distinct "personality," but it becomes part of the tree it's attached to. The following picture is of one tree with two types of plums because of grafting:

It is the same with us. If you're grafted into Jesus, the same things that flow through Him flow through you.

> Remain in me, and I will remain in you. For a branch cannot produce fruit if it is severed from the vine, and you cannot be fruitful unless you remain in me. (John 15:4 NLT)

Attach yourself to the Vine. Maybe you need the healing part of salvation, or the provision part. Speak it in. Paul and Silas made sure bitterness against their present condition didn't cause them to cut themselves off from the Vine. Their focus was their love for Jesus. The world doesn't understand that kind of commitment, nor can they explain it.

I'd say an earthquake was a pretty demonstrative and fruitful result of remaining in Jesus. I didn't include the scriptures that followed, but the jailer wanted this peace, this salvation, that Paul and Silas were a part of. Paul stopped him from killing himself over the situation he now found himself in, what with all the prisoners freed. He and his whole household were saved that night. He had listened to their faith-filled words in the songs they joyfully sang, as had the others in jail. Inner joy is a powerful force. It's our strength when we find ourselves in a tough spot. None of the prisoners vacated their cells when their chains fell off, because the Holy Spirit present that night drew them.

Abiding in the zone causes miracles to happen. It changes people. Salvation is wonderful, if you accept all it offers. Whether you're in chains in a prison or in your mind, it frees you. Sometimes people die long before they stop breathing. It doesn't have to be that way. You can be excited about your life the whole way through, no matter what. Part of the answer is found in Philippians 4:8. Like a kid, find joy in little things. Keep your mind clear of the cumbersome things.

Salvation and knowing Scripture is like the chain guard on your bicycle. It protects your pant leg from getting caught in the gears, or worse. Ultimately, it prevents unnecessary injury. (Remember Hosea 4:6a? "My people are destroyed for a lack of knowledge.") Getting your pant leg caught isn't the end of the world, but it delays you from rolling smoothly on the streets of life. God has given us Scripture as a safety mechanism. Master it like you know how to get home from wherever your bike takes you.

I know so many people, even Christians, who are downtrodden. They talk about the problems in their life, their illnesses, their ugly childhood, their victimization, and on and on. Some wear their issues like a badge of honor, calling them "*My* allergies," "*My* disease," or "*My* ______." They don't realize they're keeping those things alive by constantly rehearsing them, speaking them out and calling them theirs.

How has this system of using words as God intended so eluded the believing Christian of today? It's so simple. Perhaps it's *too* simple. As in, "How could just speaking change anything one way or another?" Yet when you become aware of the system, you'll find scriptures about words and the power of their use all over the Bible. It's like when you buy a certain kind of car. You drive it around and start to notice that same model all over the place, whereas you never noticed them before.

Surely, the freeing earthquake would not have happened if Paul and Silas had complained instead of keeping on the positive. Remember, the doors *and* the chains fell off. That's odd. That's not the normal result of an earthquake. In essence, their words went to the Father and then into the earth, so to speak, and caused it to shake them free. If Paul were a different fellow, instead of praising God in the midst of the circumstance, he might have said to Silas, "Wow. That whipping was tough, wasn't it? You know, it's so unfair. All we do for God, and this is what we get in return? Life's really hard." No, Paul knew the system and focused on the good, not the bad. Paul had been a religious man when he found truth. Truth makes you happy! The Bible says they actually rejoiced to suffer because of their faith in Jesus.

> And when they had called the apostles, and beaten them, they commanded that they should not speak in the name of Jesus, and let them go.
>
> And they departed from the presence of the council, rejoicing that they were counted worthy to suffer shame for His name.
>
> And daily in the temple, and in every house, they ceased not to teach and preach Jesus Christ. (Acts 5:40b–42 KJV)

Did Paul and Silas learn their lesson? Nope. For as soon as they were freed, they continued to teach folk about Jesus. Peter did the same thing, as recorded in the following scripture. Anytime someone tries to shut you up about your love of Jesus, this is a good scripture to remember.

> "We gave you strict orders never again to teach in this man's name!" he said. "Instead, you have filled all Jerusalem with your teaching about him, and you want to make us responsible for his death!"
>
> But Peter and the apostles replied, "We must obey God rather than any human authority." (Acts 5:28–29 NLT)

Take Charge, Tap In

Remember Philippians 4:8? Did you ever wonder why God says as a final thought to think on the positive?

> And now, dear brothers and sisters, one final thing. Fix your thoughts on what is true, and honorable, and right, and pure, and lovely, and admirable. Think about things that are excellent and worthy of praise. (Phil. 4:8 NLT)

It is because out of the abundance of your heart, your mouth will talk. Know what you know. And approve of what you know. If you intentionally *fix your thoughts* on the positive maybe things will change for you. There's a peace that follows when you know the truth.

The mind is such a follower. You can tutor it in such a way that it will work for you. Indecisiveness isn't good for brain development. Being single-minded is the key, not confused and wavering. When you hear, heed. There's no point in getting the correct instructions if you don't follow them.

> If you need wisdom, ask our generous God, and he will give it to you. He will not rebuke you for asking. But when you ask him, be sure that your faith is in God alone. Do not waver, for a person with divided loyalty is as unsettled as a wave of the sea that is blown and tossed by the

> wind. Such people should not expect to receive anything from the Lord. Their loyalty is divided between God and the world, and they are unstable in everything they do. (James 1:5–8 NLT)

"Unstable in everything they do." "Unstable in everything they do." "Unstable in everything they do." What are you feeding your tree every day? What are you grafted to? What are you saying out of your mouth that your roots are taking up? Put in the good and keep out the evil.

> And we know (understand, recognize, are conscious of, by observation and by experience) and believe (adhere to and put faith in and rely on) the love God cherishes for us. God is love, and he who dwells *and* continues in love dwells *and* continues in God, and God dwells *and* continues in him.
>
> In this [union and communion with Him] love is brought to completion *and* attains perfection with us, that we may have confidence for the day of judgment [with assurance and boldness to face Him], because as He is, so are we in this world.
>
> There is no fear in love [dread does not exist], but full-grown (complete, perfect) love turns fear out of doors *and* expels every trace of terror! For fear brings

> with it the thought of punishment, and [so] he who is afraid has not reached the full maturity of love [is not yet grown into love's complete perfection]. (1 John 4:16–18 AMP)

With this principle of speaking to yourself, rehearsing the Word, and guarding your heart, stay within the bounds of the Bible. All else just clutters your path. The Bible is a sure thing instead of just your own formulated thoughts. They will flit in and back out as the years of your life transpire, but the Word is forever. The Word of Life loves you; love Him back.

8
Salvation: The All-Inclusive Cruise

I'm an observer in life now. I can't help it. I'm still learning comparisons to God's World as I observe nature. But this chapter is not about that form of comparison, rather a different one I've been privy to as I've considered it.

I did a little research once on the origins of the all-inclusive resort. It seems the concept of this style of vacation began because it was noticed that the traveler constantly had to pay for things. It was noted that it spoiled the time of relaxation for the payer as he/she was always digging out their wallet. In addition, with the normal vacation, the overall cost could not be determined until it was over because of the variables: What will hotel rooms cost as they travel? How much for gasoline? What restaurants will be enjoyed? What excursions and activities might be experienced? etc.

The all-inclusive vacation is a package deal. It's prepaid. You pay one price at the start, and therefore you know how to save and budget for your vacation before you even get there. There's no watching how much you spend each day. Once you're in, your room and all the food and beverages are included. There are restaurants and room service to enjoy. There is generally twenty-four-hour access to the beach or pool. There are lounge chairs for sunbathing and umbrellas for shade. The resort wants you to be completely cared for. What do you need? They have it. Did you forget toothpaste?

Just go to the front desk and ask. There's even security for your safety no matter where you are on the property. They aim to please. They want you to relax.

In so many ways and in modern terms, salvation in Jesus is like an all-inclusive resort. Salvation is similar in its approach for all those who would partake. It's all-inclusive, and Jesus has already paid for it. He's bought back relationship with the Father. What loving father doesn't care for their child? The Father has even put security around you in the form of angels. There's nothing you can do to cause Him to love you less.

> But God clearly shows and proves His own love for us, by the fact that while we were still sinners, Christ died for us. (Rom. 5:8 AMP)

God knows what you have need of even better than the resort.

> Don't worry and say, "What will we eat?" or "What will we drink?" or "What will we wear?" The people who don't know God keep trying to get these things, and your Father in heaven knows you need them. Seek first God's kingdom and what God wants. Then all your other needs will be met as well. So don't worry about tomorrow, because tomorrow will have

> its own worries. Each day has enough trouble of its own. (Matt. 6:31–34 NCV)

Keeping all this in mind, what would happen if you went to the front desk every morning at the resort and asked if breakfast was included today? What would they say to you if you went there every afternoon to confirm that you have a room for that night? What would they do if you stopped by to ask how much a cola would cost? Further, what if you gathered your vacation friends on the beach, held hands, and formed a circle, praying to God, begging Him for pillows and blankets for your bed that night? It's all-inclusive! Everything is taken care of. You should have no worries that you won't have whatever it is that you need.

> Then he sent them out to tell everyone about the Kingdom of God and to heal the sick. "Take nothing for your journey," he instructed them. "Don't take a walking stick, a traveler's bag, food, money, or even a change of clothes. (Luke 9:2–3 NLT)

That's salvation. God's got you. There's not one thing you will lack, so enjoy your life. In prayer, confirm the Word and thank God for His provision, as seen in the disciples' prayer, but you don't need to beg God for that which Jesus already made sure you have. Thank Him for your life and pray for others' needs. Pray that the eyes of their understanding would be opened to see all that God has for them.

You already know it. Worry is bad for you. Anxiety is bad. Fear is a no-no with God. It brings torment, the Word says (1 John 4:18). Those are the kinds of negatives that the all-inclusive resort is trying to do away with. And so is God.

All-inclusive resorts will tell you to watch out for counterfeits. Hotels may say *inclusive*, but not *all*-inclusive. There's a difference. Many people teach a look-alike resort, a similar salvation, but not all-inclusive. The goal from the creator of the original all-inclusive was for the vacationer to put his wallet away, relax, and have a stress-free time.

> Thou wilt keep him in perfect peace, *whose mind is stayed on thee*: because he trusteth in thee. (Isa. 26:3 KJV)

So it is in this life we're living. Once we get saved, it's all-inclusive. It's so much easier to access the zone when you're relaxed and carefree.

As I paint this picture, I'm trying to broaden your mind to see something greater. What if you really believed you were on God's property and He was taking care of everything? God owns it, Jesus paid for it, and the Holy Spirit helps you walk through it and enjoy it. The concierge is the Holy Spirit. Go to His desk anytime you need direction or information. He's the Helper and the Guide. His name, Paraclete, is translated in the New Testament as the Advocate and Comforter. He's the one called to come beside you. If you fall into a hole, it's the picture of the one who jumps right down in there with you.

How do we get the rights to go on God's property and enjoy it? Faith. An all-inclusive takes care of all the needs of its rightful guests. Faith in Jesus makes you a rightful partaker of the kingdom of God.

There's a place, however, where this comparison diverges. What you're probably wondering is, "What about the people who will abuse the system?" Abuse doesn't work, since it's not born of faith. The guy who will ask for another wife or ten Cadillacs for the purpose of self-indulgence won't receive them from the grace of God. You may get what you want, but God won't bless it and you will not receive the coveted "Well done, good and faithful servant" in the end. You may be bringing a curse upon your life instead.

When you abuse the system, it brings in doubt, and the Word says you won't receive anything being double-minded. Your inner knowing will kick in when your request is born of an incorrect motive. There's no place for selfishness here. The Bible calls it carnality. Even at all-inclusives, there are parameters for the guests. You cannot abuse the property. It's best not to live outside the parameters of how God has set up the system.

If you're enjoying your resort life experience with God, why not give Him an excellent review? Tell everyone about your *stay* with Jesus Christ. You're on permanent vacation from your previous old ways of life and thinking, filled with stress, sickness, lack, depression, harmful thoughts, etc. Extend this trip for the rest of your life. Relax and "let God." When you run into a snag, trust your Father and ask Him the direction to go. Stay in the zone.

> He that spared not his own Son, but delivered him up for us all, how shall he not with Him also freely give us all things? (Rom. 8:32 KJV)

9
Going Deeper

Nowhere in the Bible does it say to read the Bible; it instructs to *study* the Word.

> Study to show thyself approved unto God, a workman that needeth not to be ashamed, rightly dividing the word of truth. (2 Tim. 2:15 KJV)

Although reading is the start, meditating and soaking up the rays all day long, as long as the sun shines, is what works best. That's what trees do, sunup to sundown. As soon as light appears, they start.

It's really digestion and breaking down the Word that counts. It makes it usable. You have to know some things in order to pull from them. Once you know it, you know it, right? Maybe not, as you'll find out further in this chapter.

Digest what's good to eat. Digestion is what moves you into growth. Your body doesn't use the nutrients from a cucumber or carrot without breaking them down first. Crushing it in your mouth comes first, and then on through an elaborate digestive system, utilizing multiple organs for the benefit of the whole body. What a picture!

Experts say you'll really know a foreign language when you start dreaming in that language. It gets deep into the subconscious. Actors rehearse lines until they practically become that character they're playing. Professional athletes rehearse a move over and over. They practice, practice, practice. They see it and sleep it. They run through it in their minds and see themselves doing it until they're dreaming about it. That's how they succeed.[3]

Are you familiar with Pistol Pete Maravich, the famous basketball player in the 1970s? As a youth, it is said, he *always* had a basketball in his hands. He carried it around town with him. His friends remember him as he spun it on his finger while ordering a malt from the soda jerk as a teenager. He developed all kinds of tricks with that basketball, because he never went anywhere without it. He knew everything about handling that ball. He had a way of getting full momentum on long shots by drawing the ball up from his side. Thus, it appeared like he was pulling a pistol out of its holster. And he was one of the greatest ballplayers that ever lived, say his peers. He died young from a heart issue that he had been born with. If they had known of it, he would never have been allowed to play.

After his career, he studied several Eastern religions in the pursuit of truth. He eventually committed his life to Jesus. He said this: "I want to be remembered as a Christian, a person that serves Him to the utmost, not as a basketball player." That's a pretty strong statement. But his example to subsequent athletes in the way he honed his gift is striking and worthy of emulating. He was a man who definitely reached his potential, both on and off the court.

We have a good friend, Fred, who plays various instruments in such a way that people gather around to hear. He has played at Disney theme parks, at NFL football games, on TV programs, and a whole host of other venues. But when he hears a statement like this one, "What a wonderful gift you have for playing piano!" he presents a surprising answer. He flatly states, "Gift nothing! When I was a kid and all the other kids were out playing, I was practicing my scales." He studied. He went deep. Now his fingers fly up and down those black-and-whites so fast you can hardly crack the code of what key he's playing in.

In construction, I've interviewed potential employees. They've said, "Oh yes, I'm experienced in roofing." But the truth is, they once put on some shingles with their grandpa. I hope you see the difference!

The Phylactery

We're talking about studying the Word here. So what does that entail exactly?

Jews even in Jesus's day had what was called a phylactery. It was a little leather pouch strapped to their forehead containing the current scripture on which they were meditating. It was their "string around the finger." If you desire to be as proficient in the Word as Pistol Pete was with a basketball, or Fred at the piano, it will take some focus.

> Follow my advice, my son; always treasure my commands. Obey my commands and live! Guard my instructions as you guard your own eyes. Tie them on your fingers as a reminder. Write them deep within your heart. (Prov. 7:1–3 NLT)

The use of a phylactery was how they learned the Old Testament scriptures, inside and out, deep down in the heart of them. They muttered that piece of information all day long. It was a determined focus. It's a little hard to ignore something that is front and center on your head.

> I will never forget your commandments, for by them you give me life. (Ps. 119:93)

You may not need to go to the length of tying something on your forehead, but the cool thing is that learning the Word isn't hard to do. It's as easy as walking. Just take a scripture or passage, read it over a couple of times in the morning, and then ponder on it throughout the day. Learning happens little by little. Beyond this introduction to the scripture, read on.

> For precept must be upon precept, precept upon precept; line upon line, line upon line; here a little, and there a little. (Isa. 28:10 KJV)

Ask God how the particular scripture applies to *you*. How can you start implementing the godly principle into your own life? Think about it. Rehearse it. Can you put your own name in it, or is it written to someone else? Don't take a scripture written to a wife when you're the husband, or vice versa. How does it fit *you*? All scripture has to be read in light of other scripture, so what are some other scriptures that round out the one you're learning?

While you're taking your morning shower, waiting at a stoplight, sitting in the waiting room, or taking a lunch break, go over that scripture out loud by muttering it to yourself. Focus. Decide. Talk to yourself about it, out loud. Then you'll know it, for life. You're already talking to yourself about something, anyway, aren't you? You're always thinking about things, going over it this way and that. You're always affirming something in your thoughts; why not make sure it's something good? It takes the same amount of effort to believe something positive as it does something negative.

Oida vs. Ginosko

I once did a word study on two of the Greek words translated in the Bible for *knowing*. The Greek words are *Ginosko* and *Oida*. *Ginosko* is a progressive learning. It may start with identifying an object, but then it progresses to more detailed knowledge. *Oida* is deeper yet. It's all-knowing. It's the God kind of knowing. God knows not only what something is but also what it is not. He *knows* faith. And He knows "lukewarm" faith. Philosophical questions about the Bible can indicate a lukewarm attitude, and that's not good in God's opinion.

> So then because thou art lukewarm, and neither cold nor hot, I will spue thee out of my mouth. (Rev. 3:16 KJV)

The problem is, we come from a culture that responds with, "I know that," but it's only by observation. How many of us have delivered a scripture to someone that we think would help them in their situation and had them respond with, "I already know that"? But apparently they don't *know* it, or they would be implementing it.

I heard it taught once that our Western view is that we think we know it because we've heard it before or have identified what it is. It's a very shallow degree of information on the subject. The Eastern and Jewish view is that you don't know it until you've *done* it.

Take a coffee table, for example. You know what that is. If Ginosko is progressive, that would be the start of Ginosko, to recognize something for what it is. But here is Oida: Who made the table? Not only what company, but also what person? Do you know what wood it's made from? Do you know from where the lumber was obtained, and how old the tree was that produced the lumber? And do you know if they used nails or screws to put it together? And glue? And do you know a thousand other things about that table? Do you see where I'm going with this? When you really *know* something, you know a tremendous amount more than just to identify it.

Do you remember (in chapter 1) me telling of the time God identified the location of the diamond ring for me to find? That's Oida. For that moment in time, He let me in on a little bit of His all-knowing. I was driving to work (for a half-hour) before He spoke that tidbit of info to me. I had been enjoying being in the zone, spending time with Him.

Be assured that the Word of God goes deep. It's able to judge every thought that comes into your head. Now that's knowing! It's like deep tilling of soil.

> For the Word that God speaks is alive and full of power [making it active, operative, energizing, and effective]; it is *sharper* than any two-edged sword, penetrating to the dividing line of the breath of life (soul) and [the immortal] spirit, and of joints and marrow [of the deepest parts of our nature], exposing and sifting and analyzing and judging the very thoughts and purposes of the heart. (Heb. 4:12 AMPC)

Having that connection to an all-knowing God can reap extreme results. Well, they're extreme in our consideration. It's what He considers normal. In my life of attempting to go deep with God and experiencing the fruit of living in the zone, I got a specific word from God that saved a man's life. God truly is omniscient and desires to include us in His all-knowing world.

I was in the zone when I perceived an urgent need to get over to my current building project instead of going to the office. No sooner did I arrive at the jobsite than the event occurred that God called me there for.

Unfortunately, God constrains me from going into detail. I had to remove the account from the first draft of the book. I don't know why exactly, but I know God has reasons for everything He instructs. But that is one day I will never forget. You see, I had inside information. I knew that God put me there expressly to prevent a complete, deadly disaster from happening.

Timing is everything with God. He is so good! He valued a man's life enough to inform me of the trouble to come.

Oh, that we would *know* that God wants to be in the middle of everything we're doing! I'm sure His attitude is that we would always keep that bit of information front and center in our thinking. He's a caring Father.

> God's various expressions of power are in action everywhere; but God himself is behind it all. Each person is given something to do that shows who God is: Everyone gets in on it, everyone benefits. All kinds of things are handed out by the Spirit, and to all kinds of people! The variety is wonderful:
>
> wise counsel
> clear understanding
> simple trust
> healing the sick
> miraculous acts
> proclamation
> distinguishing between spirits
> tongues
> interpretation of tongues.
>
> All these gifts have a common origin, but are handed out one by one by the one Spirit of God. He decides who gets what, and when. (1 Cor. 12:6–11 MSG)

10

Tilling: Rip That Soil!

Know the Word of God. And keep your heart tender toward Him. Sometimes soil can be hard ground. Have you ever used a rototiller for a garden? Keeping your heart tender can be like using a rototiller.

In the next few paragraphs, I'll attempt to do what Jesus did when comparing farming to the learning of Scripture. I might flip back and forth, factually speaking and spiritually speaking, so I hope you can keep up. Farmers plant. The comparison is enlightening as we, too, plant the Word of God in our hearts. And of course, we're not talking about the blood-pumping organ, but rather the core of who you are.

> And the seed that fell on good soil represents those who hear and accept God's word and produce a harvest of thirty, sixty, or even a hundred times as much as had been planted! (Mark 4:20 NLT)

Deeper tilling is a good thing, as we saw in the previous chapter. It's important to *know* the results of deep tilling versus shallow. Here's a farming fact that will help you visualize the tilling of the soil of your heart.

When farmers plow deeper than normal, the potential for a greater harvest is increased. Sometimes, due to deep tilling (and if conditions are right), the number of kernels on a cob of corn can *double*. Now that's an increased harvest! The end product you're looking for, after all, is the fruit, which is corn. So in the same size field with the same amount of work, you can double the harvest by plowing deeper. You can picture it; the roots of the stalk have a much easier time going deep into that softened soil. If the soil has been properly tilled, during the dry time of summer, a deeper root system spells more access to water contained in the soil.

I have an Iowa corn-farming associate and friend named Chris. I called him about plowing while putting this chapter together. I wanted to get the facts right, as so much has changed since I went to school for agribusiness. He stated that there are fifty ways to farm these days and most of them aren't incorrect, just different.

Do you listen to teaching tapes every morning while in the bathroom, getting ready? Do you have certain authors, teachers, etc. that you can understand and thereby receive well from? Are you currently going to one of the numerous Bible colleges America offers? Do you attend Christian conferences? Read self-help books? Or are you old-school and just read the Bible every day to feed your spirit the food it craves? There are fifty ways to grow spiritually, but plowing the ground of your heart seems to be universal.

Chris had an interesting term for *plowing*. He called it ripping. He said, "When you *rip* the soil, it does increase your potential for a greater harvest, but it also has some negative repercussions." It wreaks havoc with the machinery necessary to be on that field in subsequent passes. The soil is uneven. The tires get stuck in the ruts, the planter can have trouble, the rain can do crazy things in the soil, etc.

My view is that the *ripping* these big, deep plows do is equivalent to a hurricane in the ground. Yes, it's rough on it! Everything is stirred up, mixed up, and topsy-turvy. It's chaotic at first. It can be like when your lifelong, previous religious views undergo upheaval because of what you learn directly from the Word of God. It's what happened to me.

I was raised in a certain denominational church. Then I studied the Bible and found some discrepancies with what I had always believed to be true. There was a hurricane going on in my spirit for a while. I vacillated at times. I got blown around. And at other times, I locked on. I had to sort some principles out—keep some and ditch some.

Heavy loads in life can affect us negatively. We get pressed. We can develop a rough response to life when our soil isn't worked up and smooth. We do much better when we're sure of ourselves, don't we?

Being unsure of yourself is not good for the brain. For example, pressing the Snooze button on your alarm numerous times in the morning is confusing to your already-made-up mind from the night before. Grabbing a second cupcake isn't good either if you've already made up your mind to have only one. Can you visualize the uneven ground? And the scrambled mess in the brain? Pathways are started and then abandoned. Do you know people who have a hard time making decisions about things? They're usually confused about other things too.

Further, when it comes to farming, Chris described the best soil is soil that's been left alone for three years. It's soil that has been well worked up but is now smooth. He called it "mellow." It gets soft with no machinery on it. It takes a seed very well. It gets into a rhythm. An environment has been created that's perfect for planting and growth. The consistency crumbles easily in your hand. At one point, the soil reaches a stage where the no-till method of farming works.

Spiritually speaking, it's compared to you knowing the Word so well that it's just in you. You've got the rhythm of receiving Scripture and accepting it immediately into your spirit as truth without doubting its validity. You change. You plant the seed and it grows. That's it. Revelation comes, and the fruit-producing stage is reached quickly.

> By his knowledge the depths are broken up, and the clouds drop down the dew.
>
> My son, let not them depart from thine eyes: keep sound wisdom and discretion:
>
> So shall they be life unto thy soul, and grace to thy neck. (Prov. 3:20–22 KJV)
>
> My son, attend to my words; incline thine ear unto my sayings.
>
> Let them not depart from thine eyes; keep them in the midst of thine heart.
>
> For they are life unto those that find them, and health to all their flesh. (Prov. 4:20–22 KJV)

Make no mistake. As you see from these scriptures, you'll never reach the point where you don't need to lay your eyes on the Bible. But you will come to the place when you're sure about what it says. You'll make the connection between the truth you read and your response to it in your life. It will become fact to you. Then, just when you think you've arrived, more revelation comes from reading it yet again. Remember? There is one interpretation of a scripture passage but perhaps many applications of the truth it presents.

When the trials and adversities of life come (and they will), your established heart will come to bless you. What's weighty to others won't be weighty to you. You'll find you won't panic when others are losing it. You'll know answers that are so very much needed during that trial. You'll be able to procure water during the dry spells of waiting on your desired end—those things you've been praying about. It has a calming effect when you're sure that your provision will be there on time.

> They answered, "Show us a miraculous sign if you want us to believe in you. What can you do? After all, our ancestors ate manna while they journeyed through the wilderness! The Scriptures say, 'Moses gave them bread from heaven to eat.'"
>
> Jesus said, "I tell you the truth, Moses didn't give you bread from heaven. My Father did. And now he offers you the true bread from heaven." (John 6:30–32 NLT)

Apparently, they *thought* they were quoting and applying Scripture correctly, but they had it wrong. Jesus identified the true intent of the Scripture. God provides us bread to eat, which is His Word.

I had a friend named John. John was a come-beside type of friend. Suzi and I were only a couple of years into our marriage and trying to figure out the church scene and Christians and where we fit in. At a time when we were so needy for help, spiritually and otherwise, John would confirm what I was finding in the Bible. I'll come back to him in a moment.

You see, as we built our log home, we lived in it for six years without running water and electricity. We used a generator for power at times, but like the Amish living all around us, we had a gas refrigerator and a gas/wood cookstove. We took sponge baths with water we had hauled in (except for our occasional midnight dips in the numerous local lakes and rivers).

Suzi worked in town at a diner and sometimes wouldn't get home until well after dark. Having no TV and with little to do other than sit by a single lit kerosene lamp, I put myself through Bible school during those early years. I don't mean "online," as there was no such thing. I read and studied the Bible for hours and hours, thus getting quite proficient at knowing Scripture. Spread out on the kitchen table, I had my Concordance, Expository Dictionary of the Bible, Greek Lexicon, and various Bible translations in order to cross-reference what I read. Sometimes I had six books open at a time, following some rabbit trail that I found to be captivating.

We didn't want to go into debt. We built as we received money to do so. Since we were living the way that we were living, I learned by experience to trust God for *everything*. I witnessed God conduct numerous blessings, as well as actual miracles, on our behalf.

One great blessing, for example, was that Suzi received a $600 single tip one day to put toward drilling our well. God had called someone to contribute their tax return money to our need. I wish I had the pages to write all the amazing things that happened while we built, relying on God, but then it would be a thousand-page book.

Through it all, I was able to transpose many scriptures I was familiar with to a deeper kind of knowledge.

The part my friend John played was that he was my sounding board. He made sure that what I was learning, and subsequently believing, wasn't wacky or incorrect. We would talk for hours about Scripture and learn principles together. In fact, we started a Friday-morning men's Bible study, which was so enlightening, rewarding, and fun that it grew to over a dozen guys. When the Word is in you, you have to let it out! I loved talking with John and learning together with the men.

> Iron sharpeneth iron; so a man sharpeneth the countenance of his friend. (Prov. 27:17 KJV)

John helped me in so many ways. He had twenty or thirty years' experience on me. I respected him, and he respected me in return.

We both had need of firewood to heat our homes. He had the forest, the pickup, the splitter, and the chainsaw. My wife and I would pick up and load the wood he cut, then run the splitter for the big pieces. He was fast at cutting, and we were fast at gathering and stacking that truck to capacity. Then he would deliver a load for himself and a load for us. Like God's covenant with us, that seemed a little imbalanced, since he had all the resources and all we had was our youth and subsequent strength. After a few Saturdays, we both had what we needed for the winter. It was a great system of helping each other. My wife speaks fondly of those times of being in the woods and working hard.

Some years later, John had remarried and moved away. One day, I got a call from his wife that he wanted to see me. I hardly recognized him as he sat on the couch. John had been a smoker all his life. Although he believed the Word to be true and *long* outlasted what the doctors predicted for him, I believe at that point he wanted to go home to heaven.

We two reminisced at length about all sorts of things that afternoon. I found out why he called me. He had a great bitterness against his father, who had passed away many years before. I never knew about it, but it was bothering him, and he wanted help with it. I believe he felt he needed resolution there before he could feel free to pass on.

We all know what the Bible says about forgiveness. I encouraged him to forgive his dad for whatever he had done. He just couldn't get himself to say the words "I forgive" that day, even though I told him that the "feeling" of forgiveness is not what was needed in order to fulfill Scripture, only the obedience to make the choice and to prove the choice by saying it out loud. I think he took my words to heart and was able to free up those entangling roots, because John died the next day. I believe he felt the freedom to move on, and so he did.

I miss his contributions to my life. I can still see his sideways smile, and I look forward to seeing him again.

If you live to be eighty, you have nearly thirty thousand days at your disposal. What will you do with each one? Your daily habits make you who you are. Making a right choice is so important, for every choice you make has an array of consequences to follow.

I recognized I was young, just married, and building a home. I had vehicles, a job, and responsibilities. I had to make sure my decisions were good ones. I had to really *know* what I was doing. I couldn't trust that just because somebody said something, it was the truth—whether from a priest, a pastor, a boss, or a family member. That was why I started to study the Bible.

11

Having the Mind of Christ: Seeing What Others Don't See

I've heard it said that fall is the time when leaves become flowers. They turn yellow, orange, and red and cause the trees to almost look like they're on fire. The tree is saying, "I'm about to release a significant amount of potential. My leaves are about to change and drop to the ground." Just like that gorgeous, healthy tree, everybody has the potential to change the health of their core by dropping good words onto their soul. Remember, practice, practice, practice. There are those times of struggle in life when you need to drop, drop, drop leaves! Set the course for the desired end you want.

We are three-part beings: body, spirit, and soul. Your soul contains your mind, will, intellect, and emotions. It comprises your personality. It is your personal control center. And it's the soul that needs work throughout your life.

> Do not be conformed to this world (this age), [fashioned after and adapted to its external, superficial customs], but be transformed (changed) by the [entire] renewal of your mind [by its new ideals and its new attitude], so that you may prove [for yourselves] what is the good and acceptable and perfect will of God, even the thing which is good and acceptable and perfect [in His sight for you]. (Rom. 12:2 AMPC)

It's not like bull riding, where we're trying to stay on for a little bit. We are plotting a course to take this potential and ride our whole life through in a productive dimension. It takes change. No different from the caterpillar changing into the butterfly, we're shedding that cocoon and stretching our wings to fly. The soul needs to be transformed until you operate regularly with the mind of Christ. And it's the Word that does the transforming.

> For who has known or understood the mind (the counsels and purposes) of the Lord so as to guide and instruct Him and give Him knowledge? But we have the mind of Christ (the Messiah) and do

> hold the thoughts (feelings and purposes) of His heart. (1 Cor. 2:16 AMPC)

Isn't it amazing that we can hold the thoughts of Christ himself? We're joint heirs, yes. We're brothers with Him, agreed. But to actually have the mind of Christ is remarkable. That's what happens when you love someone and pursue them. You hang around them and you become like them. We know that Jesus is the Word and lived among His people (us) some two thousand years ago. Now He can live in and through us, if we would allow Him to. That's too big of a mystery for some. They don't even consider it.

> In the beginning [before all time] was the Word (Christ), and the Word was with God, and the Word was God Himself. (John 1:1 AMPC)
>
> To whom God would make known what is the riches of the glory of this mystery among the Gentiles; which is Christ in you, the hope of glory. (Col. 1:27 KJV)

It *is* a mystery. And mysteries, by their very nature, necessitate being found out, discovered, unearthed, and uncovered. That takes pursuit. Scriptural truth is only discerned spiritually. It's not understood by the natural mind. That, therefore, enters a whole other realm. But that's the realm of the zone. I believe it delights the heart of God when we press in and "discover" Him. He longs to be sought after.

Don't you? If you have someone who loves you, don't you love it when they like to be with you? Doesn't it thrill you when they spend time discovering who you are and what you like?

One of the first gifts I gave my wife after we were married a year or two was an expensive, sixty-dollar pair of gray wool pants. We still remember and smile about the story. She loved the pants, yes, but I didn't have her "mind" in the selection that I made. My wife is a practical person. We lived in the woods, meagerly at that time, without the comforts of a normal home (like plumbing!). I never considered how much she would have to spend each time to get them dry-cleaned. I never considered she would raise her eyebrows in shock when she found out how much they cost. She thanked me and definitely knew that I loved her. Nonetheless, she convinced me that it would be best to return them and put the cash into the "running-water fund," so to speak. That was more important to her. At a time when I was bringing in only $7,000/year as a carpenter, it was obvious we had other, more pressing needs.

Just like she had a different idea in mind, sometimes we can make choices that seem right and good but might not be in keeping with God's ideas. King Saul thought he was doing well when he saved out some things to sacrifice to the Lord from the people he just fought and conquered. But the mind of Christ was that he should first obey what was told to him from the prophet Samuel to destroy all. Keep in mind, I'm trying to help you learn how to live in the zone. Obedience is a key factor.

> But Samuel answered, "What pleases the Lord more: burnt offerings and sacrifices

> or obedience to his voice? It is better to obey than to sacrifice. It is better to listen to God than to offer the fat of sheep. (1 Sam. 15:22 NCV)

Living in the zone is like looking for something that you don't even know is hidden. You have to get yourself in a position to hear. Not to sound like an automated phone message, but you can say things like, "I'm ready. Here I am." The Bible says that you should open the door. He's already there. Just let Him in.

> "The people I love, I call to account—prod and correct and guide so that they'll live at their best. Up on your feet, then! About face! Run after God!
>
> "Look at me. I stand at the door. I knock. If you hear me call and open the door, I'll come right in and sit down to supper with you." (Rev. 3:19–20 MSG)

In seeking God, it might seem a bit odd that you're asking for something you don't even know exists or what the name of it is. You have to slow down, ponder, and *Selah* (Hebrew for "pause and calmly think of that"). He will speak. These are places that are not hard to find, but many just don't go there. Sometimes you have to reject and push away your past pathways and previous methods of receiving information. You have to be open to new methods, like His Spirit speaking to your spirit. It may be something totally out of the blue that He says. He's not limited to what's going on in our world. He speaks about whatever He wants. But when He does, it always brings confidence. It brings faith. It brings surety. And it displays that you're on the right track. You're like that hound dog: you've got the scent, and you're following the trail. You're almost sweeping the supernatural realm to see what's out there. But when the dog is on the scent, he has to filter through a lot of other scents on the same trail. He has to stay focused and ignore the distractions.

Did you ever watch an NFL football show where they play the bloopers and funny lines that players are caught saying during the game? They've aimed that device called a parabolic microphone to catch speech from far, far away. That's a picture of what you sometimes have to utilize with God. Just turn it in His direction. Ask Him in the midst of your day, "What do You think, God?" and He'll come back with some wonderful answer.

We can grab things that are so big! It gives you some divine insight. But it can challenge your intellect and all you've ever known and been taught. You've really got to hold on. We're just little people compared to the universe. Although we may think we're insignificant, God is interested in speaking if we're interested in listening. The right information changes everything.

> And He said, He who has ears to hear, let him be hearing [and let him consider, and comprehend]. (Mark 4:9 AMPC)
>
> Then He said, "Anyone with ears to hear should listen and understand." (Mark 4:9 NLT)

It's just so interesting how the world functions. You have huge whales the size of four doubled-up, side-by-side semis that eat thousands of tiny krill rather swallowing large fish to survive. Then you have a cheetah that takes down an animal twice its weight and carries it up a tree to survive. The world we know is not logical. Why do we think if God speaks specific things to us that it's so weird? I can tell you this: it's a place of comfort. When you tap into the Spirit of God, it's much like a baby in the mother's womb, grabbing every living resource for its life in order to grow and become like its mother. It's natural.

Having the mind of Christ—this is where it all happens, this *knowing* of scriptural truth deep down on the inside of you. This is where God breathes new life into you. This is the climax. This is the place where it all opens up to you and revelation comes. It's so much bigger than you can ever envision. This is the place of conception. You're carrying it. It's in you. You're going to have to keep on track. Don't give up that Word. Don't give up that baby, but nurture it and treat it as precious. You might have to continue speaking that God-given revelation over and over, but eventually the baby will be born. The Word will take shape, and you'll come to understand that which you did not understand before.

You'll wake up one day and ask, How did this miracle happen? It's because you stayed strong and stuck with it. It's a process, maybe not an instantaneous event. Only believe. Only trust. The truth brings freedom, and it just feels right.

That's what happened to me. My wife and I were staying at a hotel, and in the night, I rolled over and directed a thought to God in my sleepy consciousness. I said, "How did You do this, God? How have You so blessed us?" He said back to me, "Get up. Get your pad and pen. Go to the lobby, and

I will tell you." This is what he said. As fast as I could write, He spoke thus:

Trust vs. Faith
From God, 3:00 a.m., 9/24/15

Trust is what I need. Faith is what you need. Without trust, faith is shallow and weak. It's like being an amateur and you're not "all in." Once you have trust, faith is "normal." Trust is all about love, and faith is the result of that love. Trust brings about a quick response on both sides of the relationship. Trust is the key to open up the door to believe anything!

Trust stops worry and care and doubt! Trust is all about relationship. And faith is the result of that relationship. Faith can be weak and shallow and pick up some little results. And faith can also be strong and deliberate, with unique and mountain-moving results according to whatever you believe. But trust allows you to write your own ticket.

You don't need more faith; faith is as natural as anything can be. But it comes from trust—in Me and My Word.

Be a quick responder to My Word. This is your greatest exercise in life. The consequence to this is monumental. It's the first step; it's the main step. Without it, you're doomed. With it you're unlimited, only to what you believe. And now all things are possible. A baby gets what it needs, for its wants are not yet developed. A mature son gets what it needs and what it wants because he has grown up (matured). Now needs are so commonplace, and wants being met come as a result of growth, which includes character and your personal stand on the affairs of life that you have from Me [see Psalm 37:4 for clarification on that statement; it confused me at first].

That's how two are better than one. They can support each other; as each one is growing, it brings direction and stability, which brings more and better fruit, which all can see and love to see and want to see. And this is a witness for Me. I love it, like a farmer loves a spectacular harvest.

I love productivity, and I can do amazing things with so little. It's My method. It's how I do it, all the time. I only need a little bit, and that is an overstatement. Not an arm—a cell.

I love to be trusted. I love it, and it makes the whole process so easy and speedy! The greatest freedom there is is in believing. Believing Me is a joy to My heart. It's like breathing. The whole system is working. What I paid for is being received. It's not rotting on the counter. It's being used for its intended purpose.

And ye shall know the truth and the truth will make you free. (John 8:32 KJV)

Imagine, Abraham hears God's voice. God speaks to Abraham and Sarah a mind-boggling concept. He says, "Count the stars. So will your seed be" (Gen. 22:17, 26:4; Deut. 1:10, 10:22; Heb. 11:11–12). Not only is the couple currently childless but also well past the age where it's humanly possible to conceive. But God changes Abram's name, and he becomes his name's definition, Abraham, "father of many nations." They miraculously conceive a child, just as God said.

This reaction may come into your head, "Yes, but that's Abraham. Or that's David. That's Elijah. That's John the Baptist. That's the great apostle Paul. That's for someone else, not for me. Can I really tap in?" Yes! Emphatically, yes. It's already done. The faith is not that you can get God to do something; it's so you can grab on to what He's already done. It's already finished. Merely fall in line with Him.

> Peter fairly exploded with his good news: "It's God's own truth, nothing could be plainer: God plays no favorites! It makes no difference who you are or where you're from—if you want God and are ready to do as he says, the door is open. (Acts 10:34–35 MSG)

12

Living in *Sure World*: Concrete Faith

I spoke of potential in a previous chapter about tilling your soil. What I'm talking about now is like potential *plus*. When you come to believe the Word of God as the final authority, you have jumped from potential to probability. And when you get good at this, you move into what I call Sure World. You begin to operate in the zone.

> Since we consider and look not to the things that are seen but to the things that are unseen; for the things that are visible are temporal (brief and fleeting), but the things that are invisible are deathless and everlasting. (2 Cor. 4:18 AMPC)

Let me give you a visual example of Sure World. People interchange the words *concrete* and *cement*, but *concrete* is the end product and *cement* is the powder ingredient used to make it. It's the glue. Concrete consists of water, small rocks, and that all-important cement. And when you reinforce concrete with steel, like rebar and mesh, you've created something strong enough to suspend in the air and have ninety-five tons of truck drive on it. It's called a bridge.

Bridge builders must make that concrete sure. The bridge must not fall under pressure and use. It must withstand weather and climate changes, and sometimes abuse. Concrete experts know what works and what doesn't.

I worked as the construction supervisor on an Indian reservation for a few years. Every time we poured concrete, it was part of my job to take a sample to be tested. Why? It's not a good thing if the mix is wrong and the concrete gives way.

I know of something fiercely stronger than the concrete wall we call Hoover Dam that has kept the Colorado River contained for so many years. It's when your faith locks on and mixes with the Word of God that you have spoken over yourself.

> For unto us was the gospel preached, as well as unto them: but the word preached did not profit them, not being mixed with faith in them that heard it. (Heb. 4:2 KJV)

Life can be like a combination lock. When you spin that dial around and around, it's like your life doesn't lock into place. You can get confused, not knowing who you are or who you're supposed to be. But faith mixed with the Word of God is like when you enter the right combination. You hear the click of the lock come open, and you know you're in! The combination worked.

You may need some patience throughout this process, but this is the combination that makes Jesus "marvel" at someone's faith.

> And when Jesus was entered into Capernaum, there came unto him a centurion, beseeching him,
>
> And saying, Lord, my servant lieth at home sick of the palsy, grievously tormented.
>
> And Jesus saith unto him, I will come and heal him.
>
> The centurion answered and said, Lord, I am not worthy that thou shouldest come under my roof: but speak the word only, and my servant shall be healed.
>
> For I am a man under authority, having soldiers under me: and I say to this man, Go, and he goeth; and to another, Come, and he cometh; and to my servant, Do this, and he doeth it.
>
> When Jesus heard it, he marvelled, and said to them that followed, Verily I say unto you, I have not found so great faith, no, not in Israel. (Matt. 8:5–10 KJV)

Wouldn't you like that response from Jesus? Wouldn't you like it if He said to the Father about you, "Wow! Did you hear that, Father? Faith just spoke out of his/her mouth!"

When you have a selected passage of Scripture and come to believe it like a kid who jumps off the edge of the pool into his dad's arms, knowing he'll be caught, you enter Sure World. According to the Amplified Bible, a child is trusting, lowly, loving, and forgiving. And aren't they just that? Aren't we supposed to be like children? A kid doesn't think Dad will miss catching him when he jumps into his arms. God places high stock in kids!

> At about the same time, the disciples came to Jesus asking, "Who gets the highest rank in God's kingdom?"
>
> For an answer Jesus called over a child, whom he stood in the middle of the room, and said, "I'm telling you, once and for all, that unless you return to square one and start over like children, you're not even going to get a look at the kingdom, let alone get in. Whoever becomes simple and elemental again, like this child, will rank high in God's kingdom. What's more, when you receive the childlike on my account, it's the same as receiving me. (Matt. 18:1–5 MSB)

Isn't it amazing that children can have more faith than adults? It comes naturally to them. They're queued into God's system of faith already. Their brains are designed for training. They haven't been messed up by the systems of this world that drain the faith out of us. We have to get back to that state of mind when it comes to trusting Dad. We grown-ups just get "sensible" and grow out of it. After all, we have so many things to worry about now that we're all grown up, right? Not in God's system! He's the dad. The worry (which He doesn't ever engage in) and responsibility are to be His, not His kids'. How many times do we read of accounts in the Old Testament where God intervened on behalf of the children of Israel?

When no one, nothing, no event, no symptom, no evidence, and no fact can convince you to move away from the Word of God that you've studied, you form a concrete foundation for your life in that area. You have a concrete bridge to carry you across to anywhere you need to go and for anything you need to do. You've declared that the particular promise you know from the Bible is a sure thing, as far as you're concerned. There are *so* many examples of this in the Bible, but here's a good one:

> Now there was a woman who had been suffering from hemorrhages for twelve years. She had endured much under many physicians, and had spent all that she had; and she was no better, but rather grew worse.
>
> She had heard about Jesus, and came up behind him in the crowd and touched his cloak, for she said, "If I but touch his clothes, I will be made well."

> Immediately her hemorrhage stopped; and she felt in her body that she was healed of her disease.
>
> Immediately aware that power had gone forth from him, Jesus turned about in the crowd and said, "Who touched my clothes?" And his disciples said to him, "You see the crowd pressing in on you; how can you say, 'Who touched me?'" He looked all around to see who had done it.
>
> But the woman, knowing what had happened to her, came in fear and trembling, fell down before him, and told him the whole truth. He said to her, "Daughter, your faith has made you well; go in peace, and be healed of your disease." (Mark 5:25–34 NRSV)

There's so much here to study, to know, and to emulate. How can anyone deny the power contained in this passage? The woman only *heard* about Jesus. She didn't have the New Testament Bible like we do. She *said* within herself what would happen. Then the boldness—she didn't even *ask* Jesus about it! She was desperate, yes, but she chose to enter into Sure World through her faith. And Jesus was, as always, walking around in the zone. No one else perceived what had happened, but Jesus knew. No one knew what had just occurred until it was explained to them outright via Jesus's confrontation, and confirmation, with the woman.

Air is air. The same air you push into a tire is the same air that can be used to blow up a balloon or to fill your lungs for survival underwater. It's the same substance used for whatever the intended purpose. So is the Word of God. Use it for whatever is needed—for survival, for provision, for inner peace, for answers, for divine direction, for strength, or for whatever the need. Be a kid in this. Trust your dad for everything in your life.

> Trust in the Lord with all thine heart; and lean not unto thine own understanding. In all thy ways acknowledge him, and he shall direct thy paths. (Prov. 3:5–6 KJV)

Jesus told the tempter in the wilderness that we don't live by the worldly provision of bread alone, but by *every* Word that comes from God. God rescued the Israelites out of Egypt because He wanted to be their provider. He wants to be yours too.

There's a story we've heard many times that expounds on what I'm trying to explain in this chapter. It goes like this: A crowd has gathered near a river's edge at the top of a waterfall to watch a man on a tight wire walk across, risking death. He succeeds. He returns to the crowd and asks the question, "Who thinks I can cross again, carrying someone on my back?" The crowd shouts an emphatic, "Yes! Yes! We believe you can do it!" The man then points at certain individuals, saying, "Okay, I need a volunteer. How about you?" and everyone shirks back.

This story illustrates the difference between mentally assenting (agreeing) to something, which would be belief, and having complete trust. There's a vast difference between believing in God and that belief, causing you to act.

> But don't just listen to God's word. You must do what it says. Otherwise, you are only fooling yourselves. (James 1:22 NLT)

This is a colossal-size problem for American churches. They're loaded with people who attend because they believe in God but have not committed (trusted) their lives to Him. If you're having trouble understanding the difference, let me remind you that the devil believes in God but certainly doesn't trust in Him. The Bible says this:

> You believe that God is one; you do well. So do the demons believe and shudder [in terror and horror such as make a man's hair stand on end and contract the surface of his skin]! (James 2:19 AMPC)

So how do we make the transfer from belief to this place of trust? I will tell you that in life, God's wanting you to reduce your options. We have so many things in this world that pull away not only our attention but also our affections. Our heart can be fragmented into many things. Like a glass of Kool-Aid, it can get so diluted and/or convoluted that it loses all flavor. Somewhere along the line, you have to fine-tune your life. On a car engine, they put a rubber boot on the spark plug to direct the voltage to where it's supposed to go. If it were not focused, the mechanic would tell you, "It has a short somewhere. Something else is grabbing the current." We, too, should get rid of stray voltage flying around in our lives. Interests, gone unchecked, can lead our affection away from God.

Remember I spoke of the myelin sheath in the brain? It's that coating that protects predominant pathways. What pathways have myelin sheaths in your brain? If they're negative pathways, they could be what the King James version of the Bible calls "strongholds," and they must be eradicated.

> (For the weapons of our warfare are not carnal, but mighty through God to the pulling down of strong holds;)
>
> Casting down imaginations, and every high thing that exalteth itself against the knowledge of God, and bringing into captivity every thought to the obedience of Christ. (1 Cor. 10:4–5)

Here's what God says about those who exert effort to direct their own thinking, and therefore their very life.

> He who is slow to anger is better than the mighty, he who rules his [own] spirit than he who takes a city. (Prov. 16:32 AMPC)

As a teen, I was a smoker. I quit at the age of twenty-four. At some point after that, I came to the place where I couldn't even tolerate the faint drift of smoke from someone else's puff. My brain had eradicated the rock-solid pathway that had said, "I like cigarette smoke."

When I quit smoking, I thought I had arrived! I felt strong on the inside. I felt like there was nothing I couldn't conquer. It set me on the attack to see what else I could win over. What other interests in my life were taking precedence over what I wanted the priority to be, which was faith in God?

Interestingly, when a pathway is no longer needed, through disuse, it diminishes until it's gone. It gets washed away in the bloodstream and eliminated out of the body.

Yes, believing is different from trusting. Believing is simply making a choice. That's a good thing to do, but there's more to growth than that. Let me back up and expound on the actual brain function of decision-making. When you make a choice, a pathway is made in the brain. It's just a little "strand," or connection, but there is actual electrical energy used when you make a decision.

Thinking burns calories! As you use that connection, it doubles in size. As you continue to strengthen the belief by repeated use, that strand doubles and doubles again and again and again until the belief is so strong it takes some doing to remove it.

The brain was designed for information. There is no limit on its capacity, as it was originally designed by our Creator to serve us for much more than a mere hundred years. It is also one organ that repairs damage quickly and fairly easily, so feel free to place a higher demand on it. It is equal to your need or petition. Create good and godly pathways by use and repetition.

Remember, you better not listen to yourself until you speak right words into yourself. Now you have something to pull from. When you put batteries in a flashlight, you have the ability to transfer power from that reserve to the bulb when you need it. When you speak and know the right things to say, you're transferring power from the written Word of God (through the faith you have in that Word) to whatever it is you need. The words you say get energized when you *trust* in them.

A mouse can't carry an elephant, but the mouse can jump on the elephant's back and ride him everywhere it takes him. He almost *becomes* the elephant. People can look up at that mouse and say, "Who does he think he is?" But who he is is the rider of that huge nobody-messes-with animal. The Christian can be the mouse that rides God's Word throughout life. When the enemy sees us, he only sees the armor we've put on in the form of the Word of God (see Ephesians 6:11–17).

What I'm going to say next is a very slippery slope. It's one thing to read the Bible, go to church, and apply the words you hear to your life; it's another thing to take the Word of God as the central focus of your life and apply yourself *to it*. You can't throw a couple inches of topsoil on the ground and expect to change the subsoil. Although the Word of God doesn't change, it's much less effective when merely applied to your life like a Band-Aid. Do you see the difference? People get into trouble and, all of a sudden, turn to God. But the Word is to be the most immovable facet of every thought you think. Trust the Word. Again, the Word doesn't change. Paint your life on the canvas of the Word of God. It's more powerful and greater than anything you might see on this planet. It's the anchor on your boat to prevent drifting.

Why don't we realize the power of Scripture?

I had a work project once and ordered concrete. When the job was poured, I thought to myself, *Oh, good, I have a little left over. I can form up a step from this leftover concrete.* Concrete dries from the inside out. It's a chemical reaction that occurs. You can grab a shovelful of the soft outside, but as you dig deeper, eventually you will hit hard concrete. With my shovel, I found out that it had already started its chemical reaction and had set up *hard* inside the pile. That's how the Word is. When you read it, you don't realize that it's doing something on the inside of you, because your outside still seems soft and isn't showing much.

What is it you want? Speak what you want. Show what's on the inside by speaking it out. But be careful. Don't leave the flashlight on by pointing it at nothing and draining your battery. In other words, don't talk too much. Talk can be silly and wasteful. Worrying about stuff and talking about that thing you're worried about is not wisdom; it's silly talk. Give it to Dad and let Him take care of it. Always brooding on the problems of life deactivates the power of Scripture. Your will becomes confused, and you then become double-minded. The connections in your brain are muddled.

Words are like buckets that carry the power you throw out there when needed. Words are your breathing and your everyday "Word in / Word out" life when used correctly.

13

Growth: Developing Trust

We previously read in Proverbs 3:5, "Trust in the Lord with *all your heart.*" If that's the command, then there must be a way you can trust with only part of your heart. There must be a way that a person concurs with an idea but hasn't allowed it to advance to the level of trust. Someone might be that spectator who thrills over the tight-wire walker, a person who believes that one can carry a person across on his back but won't be that someone. He won't be, that is, unless he changes his belief into trust.

Believing is only part of the equation, and the first part at that. For example, you may want to buy something, but really, wanting it requires pulling out the money to make the purchase. Isn't that the significance of the following expression? "Talk is cheap. Put your money where your mouth is." Belief doesn't cost much, but trust will cost you something. You'll have to be out on a limb, so to speak, with trust. It will take you from being lukewarm to *hot.*

Trust can work both ways—trust in the negative and in the positive. For example, there are people who will say they don't believe God wants us prosperous but they work two jobs to get what they want. Oh, the lies we tell ourselves! We won't trust God (and biblical ways) to bring prosperity, but we'll certainly trust ourselves to accomplish the job. Biblical prosperity's root, after all, is in giving, not in working more. For some, the concept of working harder is easier to grasp than that of giving (sowing) and allowing God to increase finances (harvest). But God's ways are higher than ours and don't make sense to the natural mind.

> For as the heavens are higher than the earth, so are my ways higher than your ways, and my thoughts than your thoughts. (Isa. 55:9 KJV)

The maturing process is not one that just has a bunch of standards to live by—laws, rules, and dos and don'ts. That's the method used by most religions offered and created by man. It's easier on the brain to follow rules than to stretch your faith to trust that your salvation comes from one thing: what Jesus alone has done. The old covenant (law) was replaced by the new (Jesus.) Do a study and look up all the New Testament passages, where Jesus came against the Old Testament commandments to show the religious leaders that He came expressly to fulfill/replace them. In this maze we call life, following the Ten Commandments (or any of the other six-hundred-plus commandments found in the Old Testament) will never bring you closer to God or get His approval more than wholly trusting Jesus.

Growth—you can't be so stiff-necked, so black-and-white in your approach in life that you can't analyze if what you believe is correct.

> Be careful, therefore, that the light that is in you is not darkness. If then your entire body is illuminated, having no part dark, it will be wholly bright [with light], as

> when a lamp with its bright rays gives you light. (Luke 11:35–36 AMPC)

Growth, by definition, is actively increasing, expanding, progressing, and advancing. As a personal example, I have grown much over the years and have changed a very important facet of my life. I used to talk a lot and listen very little. I am now far more tuned in to listening than talking. The common expression might be, "The older you get, the more you get set in your ways," but it doesn't have to be that way. If they're negative ways, change them. Work that brain of yours. Trust the Word and work the Word.

> And Jesus increased in wisdom (in broad and full understanding) and in stature and years, and in favor with God and man. (Luke 2:52 AMPC)

A truly mature person must be able to evaluate the reality of what he says, what he believes, and what he really trusts, and whom he trusts. Then that person must make the necessary changes that will help him move ahead in life. A little self-analysis never hurt anyone.

Jesus lost a lot of followers when He introduced a new concept: that of communion.

> At this point many of His disciples turned away and deserted Him. Then Jesus

> turned to the Twelve and asked, "Are you also going to leave?" (John 6:66–67 NLT)

They couldn't grasp the idea and perceived it as having to actually drink His blood. Yet the symbolic act of taking communion is to be one of our most self-analyzing, self-correcting moments. I can see why Satan attacked it so vehemently and drove away many followers of Jesus. On the flip side, some treat the time of communion as the same old, yada-yada ritual. Communion is important. It's a time to make any necessary decision to change in your life. It's to be a time to align yourself with the Word. Even if you take communion by yourself at home, it's powerful. The Bible says, if you don't judge yourself, you could be inviting sickness and even death.

> In the same way, he took the cup of wine after supper, saying, "This cup is the new covenant between God and his people—an agreement confirmed with my blood. Do this in remembrance of me as often as you drink it." For every time you eat this bread and drink this cup, you are announcing the Lord's death until he comes again.
>
> So anyone who eats this bread or drinks this cup of the Lord unworthily is guilty of sinning against the body and blood of the Lord. That is why you should examine yourself before eating the bread and drinking the cup. For if you

> eat the bread or drink the cup without honoring the body of Christ, you are eating and drinking God's judgment upon yourself. That is why many of you are weak and sick and some have even died.
>
> But if we would examine ourselves, we would not be judged by God in this way. Yet when we are judged by the Lord, we are being disciplined so that we will not be condemned along with the world. (1 Cor. 11:26–31 NLT)

There was a time when Saul (before he became the apostle Paul) was convinced that his life's purpose was to kill Christians. In his view, they defied all he'd ever known in his Jewish faith. Saul's resolve was so strong it took Jesus knocking him off his horse, personally revealing Himself to him and blinding him with His own brightness to change that view. But the Lord prevailed against this zealous, albeit misinformed, extremist. It was a day of much trepidation when the disciples had to perform a paradigm shift themselves and accept this former enemy into the fold. God proceeded to order Saul's steps in life, and the rest is history, as the saying goes. Saul's name was changed to Paul, which means "small, humble." So essentially, Mr. Small Humble wrote a good portion of the New Testament, was an expert in the area of change, and also in how to live in Sure World. He had the mind of Christ as he wrote letters to the churches he had established. Talk about changing and growing! Truly, all things are possible with God.

A Day in the Life...

We know that Jesus's disciples weren't living in the zone at first. They had trouble stepping over the line into Sure World. Most of the time, they were dumbfounded and awed by the zone. Like good apprentices, they observed Jesus and what He did, pondered it, studied it, and asked questions about it. They spent time being spectators but hadn't yet gotten the revelation of Hebrews 11:3, where it states God created things in the universe from things that didn't exist, simply by His words. Now that's a chunk to chew and a hard system to trust, at first. Eventually, they stepped over the line from belief to trust.

The following scripture in the box (as a description of a day in the life of Jesus) was also dumbfounding, even to us who read it today.

> So they brought the boy. But when the evil spirit saw Jesus, it threw the child into a violent convulsion, and he fell to the ground, writhing and foaming at the mouth.
>
> "How long has this been happening?" Jesus asked the boy's father.
>
> He replied, "Since he was a little boy. The spirit often throws him into the fire or into water, trying to kill him. Have mercy on us and help us, if you can."
>
> "What do you mean, 'If I can'?" Jesus asked. "Anything is possible if a person believes."

> The father instantly cried out, "I do believe, but help me overcome my unbelief!"
>
> When Jesus saw that the crowd of onlookers was growing, he rebuked the evil spirit. "Listen, you spirit that makes this boy unable to hear and speak," he said. "I command you to come out of this child and never enter him again!"
>
> Then the spirit screamed and threw the boy into another violent convulsion and left him. The boy appeared to be dead. A murmur ran through the crowd as people said, "He's dead." But Jesus took him by the hand and helped him to his feet, and he stood up. (Mark 9:20–26 NLT)

Can't you just see Jesus calmly standing with His elbow on His arm and His chin in His hand, like a doctor considering the symptoms he's seeing? I mean, the boy is in the midst of a bad seizure, and Jesus calmly says, "Hmm…and how long have you been putting up with this?" What he's witnessing doesn't rile him. The true facts he sees don't seem to sway Him in any way. He knows what's in Him. He knows what He's put in there Himself. He has a concrete base from which to operate that He has formed all His life. He's seen some things. He *knows* that Scripture works. He's dropped it onto His ears and into His soil all those times He slipped away in the night to talk to His Father and receive from Him.

Did you notice in this passage that Jesus didn't pray but rather *spoke words* to the situation? And did you notice the symptoms in the boy got worse until the people said, "He's dead"? Jesus had faith and patience. This is another ingredient to Sure World. Sometimes you have to have patience—short or long, but patience.

> In order that you may not grow disinterested and become [spiritual] sluggards, but imitators, behaving as do those who through faith (by their leaning of the entire personality on God in Christ in absolute trust and confidence in His power, wisdom, and goodness) and by practice of patient endurance and waiting are [now] inheriting the promises. (Heb. 6:12 AMPC)

Like the principle in the following scripture box, Jesus just continued to stand after He said what He said. He didn't take a thought like, "Uh-oh, I guess it didn't work. My words didn't work." He waited. Jesus was standing on concrete when He took the so-called dead boy by the hand and raised him onto his feet, healed.

> Therefore put on God's complete armor, that you may be able to resist and stand your ground on the evil day [of danger], and, having done all [the crisis demands], to stand [firmly in your place].
>
> Stand therefore [hold your ground], having tightened the belt of truth around your loins and having put on the breast-

> plate of integrity and of moral rectitude and right standing with God. (Eph. 6:13–14 AMPC)

If you didn't get that the first time you read Mark 9:20–26, ask God to be able to see what you can't see. And if you said to yourself, "Well, of course! That was Jesus Himself commanding the evil spirit. I could never do that," remember what Jesus told the boy's dad: "Anything is possible if a person believes." And by that, I'm convinced Jesus meant "believe to the level of complete trust." It's very important for fathers to hear the voice of God for their families. It could mean the difference between life and death.

Here's what you have to do: don't see it the way it is, but see it the way it could be. Then you're acting like God. You're living in Sure World. You're operating from the zone. But you must listen for God's voice to speak direction to you. The knowledge of the Word that you master creates a clearer, louder voice for your life.

Listening for the Voice

I can't tell you how many times I've been directed by God not to drive here or there. I've been coached not to get on a plane or else instructed to go to the gate early. I've heard the voice of God in my spirit tell me not to sign a contract, or else to go ahead and "do the deal" with the person. I've been told to make a particular statement to someone, or even more, not to say anything at all. I've had specific words for people that meant nothing to me but everything to them.

I've given when and where God has said to and trusted Him to "refill my pot." He always has.

We've survived bad news in our finances, our health, our relationships, and basically every arena of life. I've heard the Word for my wife to such an extent that she is a new person. She respects me and turns a listening ear to what I have to say, because what I've said to her is from God. I do my best to stay in the zone, because it's become my passion to do so, not to mention how much it saves me from trouble. More and more, I seek out peace in my life because that's where I can get in the zone best. People don't know it when I'm quiet, but many times I'm trying to tune everything out and hear what God is saying to me. In America, with all we have, it can be difficult to do.

Remember what I said about God wanting to reduce our options? I don't need stuff anymore—I need God. It's so nice when we don't have to filter through all the input from TV, radio, family, work, phone, and sometimes the loudest of all, our own jumbled thoughts. Jesus was proficient at listening, even in the middle of being tussled about by a crowd of people as He walked.

> And Jesus said, Who touched me? When all denied, Peter and they that were with him said, Master, the multitude throng thee and press thee, and sayest thou, Who touched me?
>
> And Jesus said, Somebody hath touched me: for I perceive that virtue is gone out of me. (Luke 8:45–46 kjv)

I talk to myself all the time. I produce good thoughts. It's a habit I've worked to form. In fact, I've found myself to be somewhat intolerant of hanging around negative talk. One of the greatest achievements in life is the ability to go against the grain of what family, friends, and society think you should do. Instead, follow what God wants.

I speak out loud to negative situations. If anything doesn't happen the way I expect, then I trust God to turn it around so it's the best outcome possible. I work within what I know from the Word and allow God to work out the rest. I trust His judgment. It always works best. I'm very practiced at this now, and I've developed patience. I keep my focus on God. And you know what? My results are getting better and better.

> And that's not all. You will have complete and free access to God's kingdom, keys to open any and every door: no more barriers between heaven and earth, earth and heaven. A yes on earth is yes in heaven. A no on earth is no in heaven. (Matt. 16:19 MSG)

I know how much God loves me. I used to tell people, "He's got a picture of me in His wallet," just so they would get the idea of how much He considers us family. We have a back-and-forth fellowship together. It's not one-sided. In the zone, it's talking and a lot of listening. But it starts with knowing Scripture and allowing it to get deep on the inside, permeating every part of your thinking.

Sometimes people don't think about the main points; they miss them. They spend time on minor points that don't matter. One thing I learned from playing baseball and football was what my coaches said: "Keep focus. Always keep your eye on the ball. Watch the ball all the way into your hands." The ball, the ball, the ball—that's what you're after. Nothing else matters. As a wide receiver, I remember making several one-handed football catches, but I can tell you I didn't make those dramatic, reaching catches until I mastered the two-handed catch. Don't drop the ball on these principles! They're key to your life success.

14
Attitude: Lay Down That Mulch

We can't move on without touching on the subject of attitude. Of course, your positive spoken words will come to change that, and you'll most likely become a more thankful person. Thankfulness, no matter what your current circumstances, is key to possessing real joy in life. This is also the key that opens the door to changing bad circumstances into good ones. It's said that how you handle yourself in the midst of a trial has everything to do with how you come out of it. Remember Paul and Silas chained in the dungeon singing hymns? That's a definitive case of applying mulch on top of the soil holding your planted seed.

You never see an oak tree bummed out because things aren't going well. It just does what it's designed to do: grow. It does that to the utmost, taking advantage of every available resource.

Attitude seems like something you have to address early on. It's harder to deal with weeds once they've taken root and grown tall. They have to be yanked out as they can crowd out planted seeds.

You can do it. And it won't be that hard either. It's just a mindset. You put on a good attitude in the morning like a pair of pants.

> But let us, who are of the day, be sober, putting on the breastplate of faith and

> love; and for an helmet, the hope of salvation. (1 Thess. 5:8 KJV)

The day I accepted Jesus as my Savior was a great day. The day I was fully filled with Dunamis (Greek word in the Bible for *power* and where we get the word *dynamite*) from the Holy Spirit was spectacular. But I've had other life-changing experiences subsequent to those. They are Dunamis, revelatory moments. The day that 2 Corinthians 5:21 came alive to me was stupendous. That was many, many years ago, but I remember the day. It was in my "mental phylactery" for a while until I could really grasp it. Once I did, I was never the same again.

> For he hath made Him to be sin for us, who knew no sin; that we might be made the righteousness of God in Him. (2 Cor. 5:21 KJV)
>
> For our sake He made Christ [virtually] to be sin Who knew no sin, so that in *and* through Him we might become [endued with, viewed as being in, and examples of] the righteousness of God [what we ought to be, approved and acceptable and in right relationship with Him, by His goodness]. (2 Cor. 5:21 AMPC)

When I found out that righteousness wasn't based on my feelings but strictly on what Jesus did for me, my whole attitude in life changed. I ceased pondering upon all the guilt feelings for the bad stuff I'd done. I ceased comparing myself to others. I ceased the ups and downs I'd felt at times. Good news didn't necessarily bring me happiness, and bad news didn't bring me down.

Attitude can be your greatest asset or your worst downfall. Do you believe that to be true? Choosing life, as commanded in Deuteronomy 30:19, is choosing the right attitude. You can't choose life and be depressed, can you? If so, you might not be doing it right.

Attitude is like a moving system. It either moves growth in or bad stuff out. Recognize that a poor attitude could be poison you're putting down over the soil of your flowers instead of good mulch. I can tell you this: if you have children, I would discipline attitude more than behavior. Teach them to be happy, to be thankful, and to go to God with all their needs. Don't allow complaining in your home, and you'll save those little people who live with you a whole lot of grief in life when they're adults.

When my wife and I were starting out, we built that first log house together. We built it back in the woods, a half-mile off the main road. We have plentiful stories and rich testimonies of how it was built piece by piece with only $3,300 to start. It took years, and we lived in it while we worked on it. In fact, we lived there for five years without running water or electricity while building. We sacrificed many comforts while choosing to remain debt-free. The house was complete, for the most part, when it burned down. The fire trucks had a difficult time making it down the snow-covered half-mile driveway. That was one hot fire. Those solid rock elm logs burned for over a day.

Through it all, friends (who thought they knew me, but maybe not) were amazed that I maintained a positive attitude. I did my best to watch what came out of my mouth from that first phone call with the bad news that my house was ablaze, until I was sleeping in my own bed again.

That single event took years of hard work from me. It was more than a small setback when my home and everything in it disappeared in the matter of a day. And yet I waited on God, and lo and behold, the replacement log house was even better than the original, in many ways. And how very, very much I learned about life in the process of building them both! Those lessons learned are irreplaceable. That was where I was when my level slid down the wall, and I knew I should have moved it. It was where I discovered that God was interested in every fragment of my life.

Ponder this: what's the difference between 211 degrees and 212? One is very, very hot, and the other can run a locomotive across the country. My desire has always been to stay as hot as I can about the things of God. If He doesn't like an indifferent, half-hearted, lackadaisical, unenthusiastic, unexcited attitude, then neither do I.

> I know all the things you do, that you are neither hot nor cold. I wish that you were one or the other! But since you are like lukewarm water, neither hot nor cold, I will spit you out of my mouth! (Rev. 3:15–16 NLT)

Attitude—it's the mulch you put down to cover your soil. It keeps soil in excellent condition. It keeps moisture in and weeds out. Remember, attitude doesn't have to do with feelings. It's a choice you make. And if you make the choice often enough, it becomes a thought pattern that believes the best about everyone and everything. It forms a pathway in the brain that becomes the go-to path to follow.

How a good attitude comes is what we're talking about. Whatever you decide that you like or don't like, what you allow or don't allow, or what you accept or refuse sets up the parameters of a good or bad attitude. Very seldom, in the area of seedtime and harvest, does one ingredient fix so many problems. Mulch/attitude is that ingredient. Read Norman Vincent Peale's *The Power of Positive Thinking* or a host of other books to come to recognize its strength in your life, if you haven't already.

Our responsibility, or our ability to respond, is to have a good attitude, as it's your attitude that is perceived by everyone around you. Of course! They pick up on your attitude better than you do yourself. You can't hide a bad attitude. It comes out in your body language, besides your mouth.

This very thing has the ability to wreck your life.

I remember that I actually lost a friend who had harsh words for me because I wouldn't view the house-burning tragedy as a tragedy, the way most would. He said I wasn't facing reality and that I was in denial. We're not the only ones who have experienced a house fire, and we won't be the last, but I refuse to look at it as a tragedy. If someone asked me, "What tragedies have you experienced in life?" I would have to answer, "None." I've only experienced building blocks that have made me one strong, faith-filled believer in the Word of God.

God declares that I can be "like a tree planted by rivers of water" (Ps. 1:3). Is there any lack suffered by a tree in such a locale? No. I have my source for sustenance. I have taken every event and said, "I'm going to build on this…and on this…and on this." With the right attitude, you can build on anything and make it God-motivated and get it God-centered. In that way, you give Him the right to interfere in your life and change things around. It's strange to write that sentence, but it's true. He has given us choice and free will in our lives, hasn't He? Look to *Him* in the face of adversity, which is something *everyone* faces in one form or another.

There is no method that God can give you to lead a happy, fulfilled life and one that will cause you to overcome through any trial you face, if you have a bad attitude. Attitude is one of the sails that you lift up on your mast. It can be a driving force that moves your ship, one direction or another. For instance, if you don't like eating off a plate with dried egg on it, will that wreck your meal? Then your morning? Then your day? And correspondingly affect your interaction with your coworkers, your spouse, or your kids? The change that needs to be made is to respond correctly to a bad event. Ask for a new plate with a smile on your face and enjoy your day.

We're all familiar with the common expression "It's not what happens to you in life that matters, but how you respond to it."

> And we know that all things work together for good to them that love God, to them who are the called according to his purpose. (Rom. 8:28 KJV)
>
> And Joseph said unto them, Fear not: for am I in the place of God? But as for you, ye thought evil against me; but God meant it unto good, to bring to pass, as it is this day, to save much people alive. (Gen. 50:19–20 KJV)

There's no Murphy's law in God's eyes. He can turn any bad situation around, can't He? Remember, I observed that the huge tree doesn't bellyache about a storm after it's been nearly bent in half by high winds. And when it loses branches or half its leaves, it just goes about rebuilding. That's it. So when tragedy strikes, look ahead. Take on the powerful force of *hope* and move forward.

15
The Process of Growth

God hates complaining. He will bless those who are faced with tragedy in spite of its devastating effects, but the complainer cuts off God's supply by a bad attitude. God has a great response of good to our tragedy. Why waste time questioning Him or, worse, blaming Him? You won't win that way, I can tell you. He's our source for life, after all. What is a tragedy for one person is an opportunity for another. It's what separates the hearers of the Word from the doers.

> But don't just listen to God's word. You must do what it says. Otherwise, you are only fooling yourselves. (James 1:22 NLT)

It's almost like you chain yourself up if you voice negative thoughts through a bad attitude. We all do it at times. But it's like putting a kink in your garden hose. The flow wants to come but can't. Or it's like putting on grimy glasses. You look through a distorted, smudged pair of glasses by looking only at circumstances and symptoms as the end of it all. And God forbid that you would end it all, simply due to a "tragedy" that's happened in your life! If that's you and you're tempted, I implore you to wait. Give God the opportunity to turn things around. He will. I promise you. Things will not always be as they are now.

I had a friend who was a businessman. One afternoon, he popped up on my spiritual radar, and I felt I was directed by God to stop in and see him. God's timing is impeccable. I could tell by his face when he closed the office door behind me that something was up. He had just found out that he was facing financial ruin. He had made a bad business decision. He stated that he wouldn't be able to face his family or employees when his business would soon go belly-up. That morning, I talked him out of suicide as an option.

Everything in life is subject to change. God's the author of change. That event occurred many years ago, and he survived the "tragedy." He still has that successful business and a wonderful family. God got him through. He's a stronger believer and happy in life. He learned much through that terrible time of suffering. And…he smiles whenever he sees me walk through the door to engage in a brief visit.

God has given us the exciting privilege of seeing Him in the middle of anything tragic. How many testimonies have we heard of Jesus showing up just in time? And actually, He's shown up many times when it *appeared* to be too late. Read in John 11 about decomposing, four-day-dead Lazarus rising from the grave.

Truly, there is a daily fork in the road of your life. Which way will you choose to look at the events of the day? Whether it's as irritating as a badly located papercut or as upsetting as a car accident, be careful of your mouth. Don't let your thoughts take you someplace where you ought not to be going.

Life without the correct response only dulls your knife. It's very easy to see the problems in your life. It's very easy to complain and say the wrong things. Remember to set your course first thing in the morning. Put a bit in your mouth, take control, and direct your conduct.

> We get it wrong nearly every time we open our mouths. If you could find someone whose speech was perfectly true, you'd have a perfect person, in perfect control of life.
>
> A bit in the mouth of a horse controls the whole horse. A small rudder on a huge ship in the hands of a skilled captain sets a course in the face of the strongest winds. A word out of your mouth may seem of no account, but it can accomplish nearly anything—or destroy it!
>
> It only takes a spark, remember, to set off a forest fire. A careless or wrongly placed word out of your mouth can do that. By our speech we can ruin the world, turn harmony to chaos, throw mud on a reputation, send the whole world up in smoke and go up in smoke with it, smoke right from the pit of hell. (James 3:2–6 MSG)
>
> If any man among you seem to be religious, and bridleth not his tongue, but deceiveth his own heart, this man's religion is vain. (James 1:26 KJV)

With the right attitude, if surprises appear, you've already dealt with the fears and worries that can accompany them. You've declared the direction you personally will go. Subsequently, the situation cannot stick to you. Every day, when you show forth a good attitude no matter what, you're taking the opportunity to show God how much you trust Him and rely upon Him. I think He's big enough to get you through whatever you face.

You see, forty thousand men of God saw Goliath as a problem too big to solve. The *natural* way to see Goliath is that he was huge. Of course he was. Most likely, he's killed any opponent he's ever confronted. David was so confident in God he picked up five stones, as Goliath had family members that might need dealing with once he took him out. David's thought was, "Wait a second! Even giants are small when compared to God." David only saw God as big enough.

> The Philistines had a champion fighter from Gath named Goliath. He was about nine feet, four inches tall. He came out of the Philistine camp with a bronze helmet on his head and a coat of bronze armor that weighed about one hundred twenty-five pounds. (1 Sam. 17:4–5 NCV)

Developing a good attitude is part of the growth process. You cannot stay the same and grow. Suffering is in place and is a great building block in order to flow in the zone, but most people avoid it like the plague. They're always looking for Easy Street, but that's not where the action is. Everyone is looking for the easy way out, but you see very few gains and very few losses, and very little advancement there.

Understand, suffering is a godly system. In order to grow, that seed has to burst forth from the shell. That's work. That's pain. Like the chick in the egg, he has to peck through that shell on his own. So do you. No one can fight your spiritual battles. No one can defeat your inner weaknesses for you. We surely enjoy picking fruit, but it's challenging to grow it.

David suffered as a youth. As a shepherd boy and the youngest of many brothers, I'm sure, he had to work through *feelings of insignificance*. He had to work through the *fear* of huge menacing animals with large tearing teeth like the bear and the lion he fought. He had to work through the *loneliness* of being in the pasture. I'm sure he went *hungry* at times. And maybe he even got *lost*. As king, he had to work through feelings of failure, guilt, loss, revenge, lost loyalty, etc. David had to continue believing in a God he didn't see but knew existed through his Jewish heritage. But he didn't always have his faith reinforced by others. All this suffering occurred in order to bring his thinking into submission. Just as Jesus learned through what He suffered.

> Though he were a Son, yet learned he obedience by the things which he suffered. (Heb. 5:8 KJV)

Let me be clear about *how* we suffer. We suffer by standing and continuing to stand. We suffer by voluntarily putting ourselves through faith exercises, like fasting, as Jesus did. The growth process itself is suffering. It's stretching. It's going places you've never been with few answers up front. Suffering with sickness, which Jesus diligently and consistently worked to eradicate, is not the kind of suffering God desires. Why would God build automatic mechanisms (white blood cells, antibodies, platelets, etc.) into our bodies to fight off "disease" if it's sometimes His will that we suffer with it? If your focus is on your illness, how do you fulfill your purpose? Feel free to fight against that which the devil tries to bring to defeat you and kill you.

It was God and God alone that David intended to please. He laid down lyrics to songs based on experience, for all of us to own. But he wasn't writing them for us. He never knew they would be put in a book in the Holy Bible called the Psalms of David. He wrote them for God and to encourage himself in the Lord in whatever he was going through at that time, no matter what it was.

David suffered much in his life. He was an extraordinary young believer. He wrote song after song to that God He didn't see. He created words upon words, written, spoken, and sung to God. It's no wonder God chose this insignificant little boy as king to lead His people. He was one guy who was committed to following His Redeemer. He paid attention to that which was most important. Every stanza in Psalm 119 is about the written Word of God. He was emphatic on the priority of what God said, rather than what was going on around him. David truly learned how to live and breathe in the zone. It was his choice.

> Enter through the narrow gate; for wide is the gate and spacious *and* broad is the way that leads away to destruction, and many are those who are entering through it.
>
> But the gate is narrow (contracted by pressure) and the way is straitened and compressed that leads away to life, and few are those who find it. (Matt. 7:13–14 AMPC)

The narrow road is a road under pressure. It's the picture Leo Lambert, the man who discovered Ruby Falls deep in a cave near Chattanooga, Tennessee. By the time he was well into the cave, he was crawling along with rock pressing him on nearly every side. But he could hear his reward in the distance. He heard the sound of great falling water and so kept inching along. I'm sure his thought was, "Am I creeping along to my grave or the greatest discovery of my life?" He couldn't turn around. He would have had to back out, so he might as well go forward.

Faith and patience are how you inherit the promises from the Word of God. Patience is a "standing under" with expectation, not just waiting like what you do in a dentist's office. By faith, you have the promise; you're expecting its manifestation.

> And we desire for each one of you to show the same diligence [all the way through] so as to realize and enjoy the full assurance of hope until the end, so that you will not be [spiritually] sluggish, but [will instead be] imitators of those who through faith [lean on God with absolute trust and confidence in Him and in His power] and by patient endurance [even when suffering] are [now] inheriting the promises. (Heb. 6:11–12 AMP)

Yes, growth is a process. It's struggle. It's taking the necessary steps to victory, and it generally goes like this: (1) slavery (bondage to something), (2) wilderness (struggle stage), and (3) promised land (the goal.) Think about that. God's objective in this progression is for us to increase our trust in Him. It's the right response. Our biggest problem is that we don't want to suffer. The hardest suffering there is is in bringing emotions and thoughts into captivity. This is how to overcome. Once you pass the test, you don't have to take the test again. That's when control over yourself has become natural.

When a person starts a race, they get their feet tightly wedged up against that starting block so that they have unquestionable footing and the best advantage. They can push off from a sure foundation. That's the profit suffering gets you: surety.

Lifting weights builds muscle. It's hard, but the one who lifts knows the tearing and ripping he's enduring is for growth. A woman who gives birth can be suffering one day and all smiles the next. The reward for the hard work of suffering is sweet.

People think that complaining is a bad attitude, but it's really *not believing God.* Trust is the issue. It's the missing factor, and a critical one at that. You're believing in something other than God. You're believing the situation instead of your source. Without trusting God to get you through, aren't you just being like that little child who is whining because they didn't get what they wanted? Or it didn't happen the way they expected? The only thing is, you're in an adult body now. Isn't being led by feelings called carnality, not faith? If you're throwing hissy fits because something didn't go your way, aren't you acting like an adult who's still in diapers?

> And I, brethren, could not speak unto you as unto spiritual, but as unto carnal,

> even as unto babes in Christ. I have fed you with milk, and not with meat: for hitherto ye were not able to bear it, neither yet now are ye able. For ye are yet carnal: for whereas there is among you envying, and strife, and divisions, are ye not carnal, and walk as men? (1 Cor. 3:1–3 KJV)

Gear your thinking. Shift down if you are experiencing a heavy load. Take a time-out. At the same time, watch your mouth. You can expect a bad attitude when you're tired or hungry or in pain, but you've got to suffer through and watch your mouth. Talk yourself happy again. It's never as bad as it seems at first. Don't sulk. That's not getting victory over it either. Beat that carnal response to your current physical condition by speaking out, *especially* when you don't feel like it.

Here's a true-life story that demonstrates the kind of choice I'm speaking of in these chapters on growth and attitude.

We were out to eat at a restaurant once with some friends. Their two-year-old son started to whine and cry. Our friend Mary, his mother, took him to the bathroom to have a chat with him and discipline his bad attitude. It seemed a little unfair, since it was ten o'clock at night and well past his usual bedtime. He was so tired, and hungry too. So when they returned to the table, we asked her about it. Her answer amazed and taught us. She said something like, "In life, he isn't always going to have the ideal circumstances to maintain a cheerful disposition. I want him to learn early on that he has to get victory over it." We've never forgotten the lesson learned that night.

I didn't see the boy for many years but met him again when he was a teenager. My, my, he had become a fine specimen of kindness, self-discipline, godliness, and a love for God! He was so respectful as he told me of a beautiful place he had visited twice in his short life, from which his mom had called him back. That beautiful place was heaven. You see, he had died not once, but two times. He wasn't too happy about his mom calling him back the second time, but that is a story for them to tell, not me.

Nothing can stop a person with the right mental attitude, and nothing can help a person with the wrong mental attitude. Attitude is how you mentally breathe and show forth growth. You take information in and breathe out your life, but it's always filtered through attitude. Hopefully in the breathing process, you change. That's how you grow. Examine your own thoughts—are they godly? Hang happy pictures on your walls at home. Be positive. Watch growth-producing, life-boosting, encouraging programs on TV that spark your imagination. That will help you become who God has created you to be.

16
The Power of 0.039 Inches!

> The Lord answered, "If you had faith even as small as a mustard seed, you could say to this mulberry tree, 'May you be uprooted and be planted in the sea,' and it would obey you!" (Luke 17:6 NLT)

How big is a mustard seed? It is between 0.039 inches and 0.079 inches. That's pretty small.

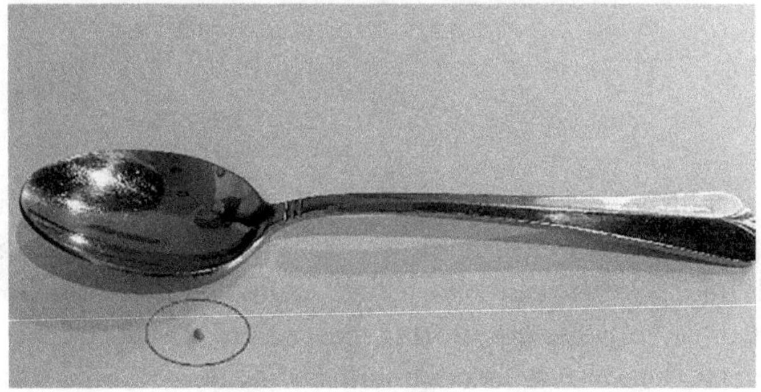

When we were first married, my wife was allergic to many things. She had hay fever and asthma, along with some skin issues. We took a stand against those things as we started to learn the Word together. I "prayed" for her many times in the night when I would wake up and hear her wheezing as she slept. I have the word *prayed* in quotes because I didn't ask God about it. I didn't ask Him to take care of it. I already knew what the Bible says about sickness and disease. I knew how much time and effort Jesus spent coming against all of it. I had put myself in agreement with God on that subject. So I said, "No, devil. We do not accept this. You take away all these allergies from her, in the name of Jesus." Today, she remains allergy-free.

> How God anointed Jesus of Nazareth with the Holy Ghost and with power; who went about doing good, and healing all that were oppressed of the devil; for God was with Him. (Acts 10:38 KJV)
>
> O Lord, if you heal me, I will be truly healed; if you save me, I will be truly saved. My praises are for you alone! (Jer. 17:14 NLT)

This is an important chapter. I hope I can be clear in its delivery. Believers sometimes think once you get enough faith, God can act on your behalf. I don't believe that's how it works. Hear me out on this. Let me explain what I mean by that. The phrase "enough faith" is the one I have trouble with. Some things are either/or. If you have a spouse, do you have a little faith that you're married, or a lot? See what I mean? Faith cannot be considered to be in levels. Now you may believe sometimes and have doubts at other times, but again my point is that it's an either/or type of thing.

How much is enough faith? For a fact, a mustard seed is pretty small (as presented in Matthew 17:20 later in this chapter in a scripture box).

First thing, when Jesus died on the cross and said, "It is finished," the system was complete. Water is always wet. Just like water comes with "the wet," it's a done deal. Whether it's a drop or the ocean, it's wet. That's the way it is. Further, if you stick a seed in the ground and water it, it will grow. It's a system. Speak the Word of God in faith and it will work. It's a system. It took a little while to see all the manifestations of my wife's healing, but eventually she came to live free from allergy's grip.

We almost trick ourselves or sabotage our own prayers by thinking that we didn't do this or that well enough to be rewarded with an answer to our prayer. Then you have those who think they did very well in this or that and therefore deserve an answer to their prayer. Either way, it's self-righteousness. Believing less or more than what the Word says about you is a form of self-righteousness.

> For I say, through the grace given unto me, to every man that is among you, not to think of himself more highly than he ought to think; but to think soberly, according as God hath dealt *to every man the measure of faith.* (Rom. 12:3 KJV)

We're so good at making up our own rules. The Father is more about relationship than adhering to a set of rules. Isn't that the whole point of replacing commandments with

His Son and standing behind what He accomplished? That was *his* decision, not ours.

> Of his own will begat he us with the word of truth, that we should be a kind of first-fruits of his creatures. (James 1:18 KJV)

We, as God's people, couldn't make it with the rules from Old Testament days. And we can't make it now without standing behind our go-between, the Savior. The religious leaders in Jesus's day were constantly amiss in their approach to Him, trying to catch Him up on breaking the commandments (or whatever law was given in the Old Testament—read Matthew chapters 21–23). But Jesus has established new rules of faith in God. Those are the ones we are to adhere to. Are they different? Somewhat. I would say it like this: Jesus encapsulated the old with His new. For example, He Himself replaced the Sabbath. Jesus became the rest we are to enter into according to the fourth commandment. Without going too deeply into this, here's what Jesus said about whether he was replacing the old or adding to it.

> "No one sews a patch of unshrunk (new) cloth on an old garment; otherwise the patch pulls away from it, the new from the old, and the tear becomes worse. No one puts new wine into old wineskins; otherwise the [fermenting] wine will [expand and] burst the skins, and the wine is lost as well as the wineskins. But

> new wine must be put into new wine-skins." (Mark 2:21–22 AMPC)
>
> Then Jesus said to the Pharisees, "The Sabbath day was made to help people; they were not made to be ruled by the Sabbath day. So then, the Son of Man is Lord even of the Sabbath day." (Mark 2:27–28 NCV)

James said, "Show me your faith by your works." But the works are not intended to get something from God. Works are a result of love but not to *get* love. Our works are a natural result of our love for Him and our faith in Him. You love your child because he's your child, not because he cleaned his room.

> Now someone may argue, "Some people have faith; others have good deeds." But I say, "How can you show me your faith if you don't have good deeds? I will show you my faith by my good deeds." (James 2:18 NLT)

If we make a mistake, if we sin, we ask forgiveness and move on. There's no atonement necessary, no penance and no beating yourself up about it. Ask forgiveness, and just like you trusted that you received salvation by going to Jesus, trust that you are indeed forgiven by confessing the sin and repenting of it (turning away from it). And go to Him for the release of the guilt of it. It's essential to keep a clean heart.

> If we confess our sins, he is faithful and just to forgive us our sins, and to cleanse us from all unrighteousness. (1 John 1:9 KJV)

One thing I've always been good at, my wife says, is avoiding self-condemnation. That's because I meditate upon 2 Corinthians 5:21, spoken of in a previous chapter. I do my best to say, feel, act on, talk about, think on, and do what's right. Beyond that, I go to God. God created the brain. Did you know that guilt, shame, and condemnation are not good for the brain? Read Dr. Caroline Leaf's book *Who Switched Off My Brain?: Controlling Toxic Thoughts and Emotions* or a host of other books to find out more. Scientists are always finding out what is already a principle from the Word. I know I'll miss the mark sometimes, and for that, I have Jesus.

> You may believe there's nothing wrong with what you are doing, but keep it between yourself and God. Blessed are those who don't feel guilty for doing something they have decided is right. (Rom. 14:22 NLT)
>
> Hast thou faith? Have it to thyself before God. Happy is he that condemneth not

> himself in that thing which he alloweth. (Rom. 14:22 KJV)
>
> Your own mouth condemns you, and not I; yes, your own lips testify against you. (Job 15:6 AMPC)

If New Testament scriptures don't condemn people for eating meat or not eating meat, or for celebrating holidays or not, why do we? Do what you feel is right and let others do the same. To their own master (God), they answer.

You don't earn an answer to your prayers by what you do or don't do. The enemy is there to convince us that we're not worthy, or that we *are* worthy, because of what we do. That's deception. It's about what Jesus did. All we have to do is trust Him. Our job is to believe Him and what He taught. He's the door. He's the way.

> Jesus told them, "This is the only work God wants from you: Believe in the one He has sent." (John 6:29 NLT)

Of course, if you believe in Him and love Him, that will change your behavior. But speak His Words and don't give in. That's your part to play. Keep speaking. It's an action verb. Luke 11:9 in the Amplified Bile goes like this: "Ask and keep on asking and it shall be given you; seek and keep on seeking and you shall find; knock and keep on knocking and the door shall be opened to you." I like to say, "Speak, and keep on speaking."

Did you know that Jesus Himself had to speak more than once in order to get the desired result in a particular situation? It's recorded in the following scriptural passage:

> When they arrived at Bethsaida, some people brought a blind man to Jesus, and they begged him to touch the man and heal him. Jesus took the blind man by the hand and led him out of the village. Then, spitting on the man's eyes, he laid his hands on him and asked, "Can you see anything now?"
>
> The man looked around. "Yes," he said, "I see people, but I can't see them very clearly. They look like trees walking around."
>
> Then Jesus placed his hands on the man's eyes again, and his eyes were opened. His sight was completely restored, and he could see everything clearly. (Mark 8:22–25 NLT)

Since it's Bethsaida where this occurred (and Jesus had some things to say about that city's lack of faith in Luke 10:13), I can only imagine that Jesus pulled the man out past the city limits to get the results needed, to get away from the unbelieving.

It's interesting that as you get to know Him, you'll also get to know His voice. Much like a mother knows her own baby's cry among many, you'll pick out His voice among the hubbub of life. He's always been speaking; you just weren't hearing. He'll repeat what you already know from Scripture.

He'll confirm it. He'll remind you of His truths, and you'll hear things like this: "Don't worry. I'm in the middle of this current trouble you're having. You're going to be okay. I'll get you through it." That will motivate you to dig deeper. You'll want to hear more. You'll want to run to a quiet place and enter the zone and shut everything else out. That voice brings peace in every storm. This is why a child likes to hold a grown-up's hand. It's a place of comfort, ease, security. and validation. It's a sanctuary. And it certainly indicates a close association with the one whose hand you're holding. Just hold His hand.

We're all looking for peace, but it comes through knowing His Word. It's not from knowing just His name but His character, His way of doing things, and His love. At the point of obtaining that knowledge, this becomes a monumental moment. The world and all it offers shrinks, and at the same time, the Spirit of God increases in your life. Some call it growing, some call it maturing; we call it living in the zone. You'll find certain interests dropping out of your life and new ones coming in.

Sometimes I hear folks talk and give themselves the proverbial pat on the back by saying, "Well, I go to church." It's got to be deeper. Going to church is not the end-all. It's an ingredient in the bread, but it isn't the bread. And if you're going to a church that doesn't preach the uncompromised Word of God, you're doing more harm to yourself than good by feeding on doubt and unbelief every week. Going to church for many in America is the "status quo." It's just what you do if you call yourself a Christian. But beware: you could become lukewarm and, in fact, unbelieving.

You don't get points from God for being a churchgoer. You go to the bank and make a withdrawal because you have put money in your account, not because you're tall, pretty, smart, or strong, or because you're needy, broke, worried, or desperate. You get to retrieve that money because your name is on the account. It's yours. That's the system that is in place there.

It's no different from owning a car. It's in the garage. Go open the door, put the key in the ignition, turn it, and let that car take you where you want to go. It's your car. You own the title deed to that car. Drive it. It's another system in place. If you have faith, use it. There's a saying: "Going to church doesn't make you a Christian any more than standing in the garage makes you a car."

In God's system, prayer is answered because of your faith in Him and in His Word, not because you're needy or desperate. You're making the Word of God yours. Don't wallow in unbelief. It's a very unpleasant place to live.

> Then came the disciples to Jesus apart, and said, Why could not we cast him out? And Jesus said unto them, Because of your unbelief: for verily I say unto you, If ye have faith as a grain of mustard seed, ye shall say unto this mountain, Remove hence to yonder place; and it shall remove; and nothing shall be impossible unto you. (Matt. 17:19–20 KJV)

Wow. That's quite a principle Jesus is teaching us, His believers. If you don't already know God loves you and really, really, really loves you and wants to care for you, you're wasting a lot of time praying useless prayers instead of claiming what's already yours. Don't be timid. Boldness in faith is what pleases God. If it's a promise in the Word, it's yours.

> Therefore I tell you, stop being perpetually uneasy (anxious and worried) about your life, what you shall eat *or what you shall drink*; or about your body, what you shall put on. Is not life greater [in quality] than food, and the body [far above and more excellent] than clothing?
>
> Look at the birds of the air; they neither sow nor reap nor gather into barns, and yet your heavenly Father keeps feeding them. Are you not worth much more than they?
>
> And who of you by worrying *and* being anxious can add one unit of mea-

sure (cubit) to his stature *or* to the span of his life?

And why should you be anxious about clothes? Consider the lilies of the field *and* learn thoroughly how they grow; they neither toil nor spin.

Yet I tell you, even Solomon in all his magnificence (excellence, dignity, and grace) was not arrayed like one of these.

But if God so clothes the grass of the field, which today is alive *and* green and tomorrow is tossed into the furnace, will He not much more surely clothe you, O you of little faith?

Therefore do not worry *and* be anxious, saying, "What are we going to have to eat?" or, "What are we going to have to drink?" or, "What are we going to have to wear?"

For the Gentiles (heathen) wish for *and* crave *and* diligently seek all these things, and your heavenly Father knows well that you need them all.

But seek (aim at and strive after) first of all His kingdom and His righteousness (His way of doing and being right), and then all these things taken together will be given you besides.

So do not worry *or* be anxious about tomorrow, for tomorrow will have worries *and* anxieties of its own. Sufficient for each day is its own trouble. (Matt. 6:25–34 AMPC)

Verse number 33 says to go after God. That's all. How do you seek Him? You get to know His Word. And you display your faith in that Word by speaking it and doing it.

I'm just not convinced that God and Jesus are up in heaven with some kind of Geiger counter measuring your faith level. They're not saying, "Oh, look! He's up to number 7. A little bit more and we can give him what he wants!"

The system is there to use. Faith wasn't really meant to be measured. It's either/or. Ten thousand half-truths will never add up to one truth. You don't work faith up. You have it or you don't. A diamond is a diamond or it's not. There's no such thing as a partial diamond. One may have more inclusions than another, but they're both still diamonds. You believe God or you don't. You believe *all* the Word of God is true or not. When Jesus said, "Oh, you of little faith," I don't think He meant you have a small amount. My belief is that He meant that you believe Me in this, but you won't carry it through to that. You won't use the system in its entirety. That tiny, tiny mustard seed doesn't get bigger, but the tree it produces is huge. That tiny seed is more than enough for any situation. You must realize how potent faith is!

Segmented Faith

Here's the crux of this chapter: Is it a measurable amount of faith that God gives? Or is it just "the measure" needed? I have found in my own life, when things aren't panning out the way I've prayed, I never blame the Word or God. Rather, it's that I have to grow. First, I make sure that what I'm praying for lines up with Scripture, and I get those scriptures in my mouth. Then I make sure I believe them 100 percent, without doubting. When you're sure, you know it. Getting to know Scripture ignites faith. Now seed and soil join together like brick and mortar.

I have found that many Christians have segmented faith. In other words, they take the parts out of the Bible that they have an easy time believing and seemingly let other areas slip.

In the following passage, Jesus said to His disciples, "Oh, you of little faith," since they woke Him up fearing their death from a storm. I can promise you, when Jesus says, "Let's go over to the other side," you're going over to the other side! So don't worry. If Jesus said it, you can be assured it's locked in the vault. It will happen the way He says it will.

It might seem a little unfair how He scolded them for their lack of faith. They had never seen His faith calm a storm before. But they had seen Him feed thousands of people using a single lunch. They had witnessed the healings. They had experienced slipping through the gathering unruly crowds unnoticed. And they had been privy to many other miracles. In fact, in everything Jesus did, He succeeded. So His feeling was like this: "How is it that you still don't believe? You believe this because you saw it. Why won't you have faith in Me? Why won't you carry it through to this other need? Getting to the other side." There's the fine line I was referring to: You believe in this. Why won't you carry it through to that? Jesus was a man just like them. He never said, "This is just for me to know." He never declared, "Only I can do this." He was always demonstrating how to get the job done.

> As evening came, Jesus said to his disciples, "Let's cross to the other side of the lake."

> So they took Jesus in the boat and started out, leaving the crowds behind (although other boats followed).
>
> But soon a fierce storm came up. High waves were breaking into the boat, and it began to fill with water.
>
> Jesus was sleeping at the back of the boat with his head on a cushion. The disciples woke him up, shouting, "Teacher, don't you care that we're going to drown?"
>
> When Jesus woke up, he rebuked the wind and said to the waves, "Silence! Be still!" Suddenly the wind stopped, and there was a great calm.
>
> Then he asked them, "Why are you afraid? Do you still have no faith?"
>
> The disciples were absolutely terrified. "Who is this man?" they asked each other. "Even the wind and waves obey him!" (Mark 4:35–41 NLT)

Number 1, they're in a boat with Jesus. Yes, it looked bad, but did they really think *He*, Jesus, was going to drown?

Number 2, Jesus had just taught about how the mustard seed is the smallest of all seeds yet that it's enough when it comes to faith. He had given them the authority. Why weren't they using it against the storm, or whatever the need?

You need Scripture. You need to find out what is yours to have, as far as principles to live by. Say the Word, believe the Word, know it's from God, speak it out, and the mountain will be moved. God made a huge sacrifice to get that system in place for us. Just implement it. But don't complain to

God about the mountain. Talk to the mountain—the sickness, the financial deficit, the devastating news, or whatever the setback. Tell it what you, a faith-filled, mighty-warrior, mountain-moving, believing Christian demand that it do!

Remember, I started reading (then studying) the Word every night in the dimly lit basement of our log home being built. What I was reading got me so excited that I had to start that men's Bible study to talk with others about it.

Getting to really *know* the Word of God is like when you see smoke from a volcano—you know something's happening. Ash starts to spew out from the open hole on top. Then one day, lava starts flowing down the side and you know the mountain has erupted. Now it takes full precedence. Everything and everybody better get out of the way because it's alive and active. And with faith, there's a moment when the zenith is reached. The connection is made between your spirit and the godly principle. You get it. You really get it. You realize the impact of that particular scripture you've been mulling over, and you enter the zone through that door. It's exhilarating.

> The Scriptures tell us, "The first man, Adam, became a living person." But the last Adam—that is, Christ—is a life-giving Spirit. (1 Cor. 15:45 NLT)

This is the very thing the first Adam lost in the garden. Adam walked every day with the Father, and they communed together. He was always in the zone. He was in God's intended position for mankind, being tuned in to His voice. God had breathed His very own breath into man. Jesus is that very Living Word breathed into us. Living in the zone is all about relationship. You develop a relationship and a love for the Word, as He has set you free.

I was helping a guy work on his log home on a Saturday and stepped in a hole, turning my ankle. We both heard it crack. I could put no weight on it, and I knew it was broken. I got myself home and hobbled inside. I called it healed several times, but the swelling was getting worse. The pain was so excruciating that I vomited. As I crawled into bed, I asked my wife to call the doctor's office and see about an appointment.

I never followed through on that doctor's appointment. Jesus healed everyone, the Word says over and over in the four gospels. Why would I think He wouldn't heal me? As I lay in bed, I got belligerent about my predicament. I was angry and dished out my wrath upon the one who deserved it—the enemy. I spoke to the mountain.

The last thing I said before I dropped off to sleep was something like this: "I don't care what it looks like, devil. I know the Word. It says Jesus heals. As for me, I take that to be the truth. I'm healed in the name of Jesus, and that's all there is to it. My ankle may look bad and I may be in pain, but I'm still healed. And that's final."

The Word took effect while I slept. I got up, and I was indeed healed. I played a great game Tuesday night at our softball game when I took my position at third base.

17 The Seed

A planted tomato seed comes up as a tomato plant, never a corn plant. What seed are you? You have to *know* who you are. There's no *luck* in this, and there are no options.

My wife has a friend named Annie. Annie was adopted, and yet it's clear to her and all who know her of what seed she is and what her gifting is. She's got an inborn knack in working with horses.

Once, she was at a horse show and witnessed some people having trouble getting their horse into the trailer to go home. The more they tried, the more the horse refused. He got up to the point of walking onto the ramp but then threw a fit and fiercely backed up. All parties involved were getting more and more frustrated. With great confidence and a solution that only comes when you *know* your gift, Annie walked up to the exasperated people and offered her know-how. She said, "Is it worth $100 for you to get your horse home? Because I will bet you that I can get him into that trailer within ten minutes." They took one look at her small frame and another look at the wild-eyed horse and decided to take on her bet.

Annie walked up to the horse, stroked its neck, and got acquainted. Then she took him by the reins and walked him away from the source of his anxiety. She walked him around the back of the stables, talking easily to him. When they had gone once around, she walked right past the trailer ramp and went around a second time. Yet a third time she went around with the horse in tow, but as she approached the ramp, together the two walked right up into the trailer. Know-how.

The horse owners looked astounded and gladly handed over the promised $100. Annie tucked her earnings into her jeans pocket with a smile and said, "Glad to help you folks out!" For her, it was just common horse sense. Didn't everyone know what she knew to do? When you move within your gifting, you will leave others in awe and be rewarded for your understanding of the subject. It's a God thing. It's in the seed.

In the scripture box below, Potiphar recognized Joseph's administrative skills. That was the seed from which Joseph came. God blessed him with an inordinate ability to organize matters of life, business, finance, infrastructure, and who knows what all? Present a problem to Joseph and he would be able to deduce the best course of action to resolve it. It was part of the blessing God put on his life. Joseph's natural,

God-given knowledge mixed with God's favor equaled a life of victory. He operated in the zone.

> The Lord was with Joseph, so he succeeded in everything he did as he served in the home of his Egyptian master. *Potiphar noticed this* and realized that the Lord was with Joseph, giving him success in everything he did. This pleased Potiphar, so he soon made Joseph his personal attendant. He put him in charge of his entire household and everything he owned. From the day Joseph was put in charge of his master's household and property, the Lord began to bless Potiphar's household for Joseph's sake. All his household affairs ran smoothly, and his crops and livestock flourished. So Potiphar gave Joseph complete administrative responsibility over everything he owned. With Joseph there, he didn't worry about a thing—except what kind of food to eat! (Gen. 39:2–6 NLT)

The Israelites came to know the "skill" of the prophets in accurately hearing the voice of God. Even the Philistines were forced to recognize Samson's anointed strength and skill with a donkey jawbone (Judges 15:15)! When you come to really know your God-given gifting and move within it, your potential can be realized and you will be the most successful.

A seed is remarkable. Did you know that a seed is one thing on earth that has not been able to be artificially duplicated? Hybridized, yes. Uniquely created, no. Did you know that seeds have been recovered from Egyptian tombs and have germinated after thousands of years of dormancy? Did you know there is a variety of pine cone that releases its seeds only when there has been a fire? God has thought of everything.

Seed is potential. A pine cone lying on the ground is also a forest. *Potential*'s definition is "dormant power, hidden strength, untapped ability, or unused success," according to *Maximizing Your Potential* by Dr. Myles Monroe. For you, it could be buried treasure. It is *who* you really are wrapped inside your outer package. It's what you can do but haven't accomplished yet.

Have you come to know your particular gifting? If not, make a list of things you're good at. That's a starting place. Then give it to God. He'll reveal to you where to go with that gifting, step by individual step. Your particular gifting will create income for you at the very least. Like for Annie, it will become horse "cents" for you to move in your gifting. It will bring you satisfaction in life. It will give peace and a place from which to happily give to others.

> A man's gift maketh room for him, and bringeth him before great men. (Prov. 18:16 KJV)

Don't we all enjoy watching someone who's really good at what they do? Whether it's a football running back pushing his way through opposing players, an artist blowing heated glass into something colorful and beautiful, a ballerina spinning on her toes, or a mountain climber hanging by two fingers as he scales the underside of a rocky mountain cliff, we enjoy seeing the expertise of others.

When my wife was in high school, she took an aptitude test before college to help point her in the direction of her own propensity. The test, for her, pointed to clerical work. She took Typing I and excelled in it, but when it came to Typing II, she couldn't imagine herself typing business letters for someone as a career. She wanted a more grand and glorious *bent*, so she developed a disdain for being put in the category of clerical work.

Now that she's satisfied and established in life, what will she stay up until midnight doing with a high intensity of interest and focus? Clerical work. She's balancing a checkbook, making entries, filing and paying bills, creating invoices, and yes, typing business letters for me. That's been a blessing to me and has helped me keep focus on *my* gift. I guess the high school test was right after all. Here's what she has concluded: *You like what you're good at, and you're good at what you like.* It's all in the seed. You can't make a corn plant from a tomato seed.

Focus

Focus in life is huge. It's not *only* about getting into the ground as a seed, but that's the starting place. A seed remains dormant as long as it's a hard-shelled little container holding its possibilities. The seed has a predisposition but remains a seed until it's able, under the right conditions, to burst forth and grow. A plant, any plant, is bent on one thing and one thing only: growing. Everything it does is *only* about that. And when it's comfortable with that, the fruit comes.

Remember, the river makes the riverbank, but the banks hold the river. You might think a wide river is best, but the only time you get power is when you narrow the focus of the water. Then and only then can you harness it for power. The narrow road leads to life; the wide road leads to destruction. Any CEO or corporate manager will tell you that focus, not multitasking, gets a job done best.

Cemeteries are loaded with wonderful seeds that were never properly planted and never grew into a full productive plant. Maybe they grew a stalk but never came to be the full corn in the ear. Some seeds never even germinated. And of course, I'm talking about people here, not plants. The person lived his or her whole life and never stepped into their destiny. When you think about the seed, the explosive word that applies is *potential*. And when you think about potential, it means possibility, but not absolute fulfillment.

So who are you? Are you living in the zone as much as possible? Are you on the path your Creator intended? God has invested into you. His seed is in you. He breathed the very breath of life into you. He is the manufacturer. You can't afford to trust others to tell you who you are. Beware of what others think of you and say to or about you. Watch out. Their opinions will be skewed. Ask God.

> If you need wisdom, ask our generous God, and He will give it to you. He will not rebuke you for asking. (James 1:5 NLT)

I like to go fishing on occasion. There have been many times I have taken the boat out, found my desired spot, dropped the anchor, and cast my line. Happy in my own thoughts, enjoying the day and communing with God, after some time, I look up and notice I've drifted far away from my original spot. Choppy waters? you ask. Waves from other boaters? Forget to drop that anchor? That's a no on all counts. Even in calm waters and with an anchor to hold me, I have drifted. The gentle, unnoticed flow of water dragged my anchor (my foundation) in the soft sand in a direction I did not choose to go. That's how subtle drifting in life can be when you hang around those who are not worthy or supportive of your gifting, stated beliefs, foundations for living, and godly revelations.

When you don't know who you are, you don't need to be focused. You've heard the saying "Any road will take you there if you don't know where you're going." Don't allow yourself to drift through life. Take charge. Choose your direction, or like so many in the cemetery, it will be automatically chosen for you. The world will form you into its mold like a popsicle in the freezer. Spending all your physical and emotional energy trying to please others instead of the one who created you is draining. It's the biggest counterfeit operation of all.

I've commented previously on the life of George Washington Carver. We're still reading about him today because he was a man driven and intensely focused in his gifting from God. He was a highly successful man. If he was onto something, he knew he couldn't be sidetracked by anyone, even his coworkers (his handpicked lab technicians). That's focus! His time and calling from God were too valuable, and he guarded it as such. In the laboratory, he was living in the zone. It was a zone that God gave him. He reported that he never guessed at what to do. In other words, he never conducted experiments to see what would result based on a hypothesis. God told him what to do, which then was not an experiment at all. That was how he operated from the zone.

Jesus might have *seemed* to drift in life, walking from town to town, but He was highly focused in His direction and purpose wherever He was. He stated that He only does what He hears His Father say to do. And for us, we can't do anything apart from the Vine where we are attached to Jesus.

> But Jesus said, "I tell you the truth, the Son can do nothing alone. The Son does only what He sees the Father doing, because the Son does whatever the Father does." (John 5:19 NLT)

Absolutes

You see, there are "absolutes" in life. The Word of God contains all sorts of absolutes; just read the book of Proverbs and you'll find bunches of them. The main absolute for Jesus is contained in this scripture that says He only did what the Father does. That's it. Simple. Now, He had studied the Old Testament as a boy and was well familiar of what the Father's character consisted. He had "observed" Him all His life. He now heard the Father's voice as He lived, moved, thought, talked to Him, and traveled in ministry. Oh yes, Jesus lived in the zone. He operated from the zone at all times.

Jesus put people out of His presence when He sensed seeds of doubt and unbelief. And remember, don't feel badly about doing the same in your life. One bad apple in a bushel of many can rot the whole bunch. But one good apple doesn't make the whole lot good. Do you see the difference? You better pull that good apple out before it gets the rot too. It's a spiritual law: a little leaven leavens the whole lump. Remember Mark 5:38–42, where Jesus put the doubters (mourners, lamenters, scoffers, and negative folk) out in order to focus on getting the dead girl healed?

Jesus was so tapped into the source of His existence that there was no way He was going to drift. His anchor never dragged along in the sand in the slightest.

We've talked about concrete before. It's an amazing invention. Mix a bag of cement with a little sand, pebbles, and water and you have one solid material. Take the little parts of your life and add the absolutes from the Word of God and you will have a similar foundation. Did you ever consider that there are parts of your life that you can mix with absolutes? Like your particular personality and your gifts? Make your abuse, victimization, pain, struggles, and subsequent victories powerful by adding the absolutes from the Word of God. Cement is the part that makes concrete hard. It's the hardening component that makes the sand/pebbles plus the water unable, now, to shift.

Trials must be used correctly. They can easily be used incorrectly to make you feel like you got the short end, cheated in life. But those who use their trial correctly will overcome the negative effects and use the trial, for instance, to make their roots go deeper. Most people cringe under trials. They run from them. If you can learn to excel in trials, why, you're a more mature person than most! If you look at any scar, that skin has become tougher.

> Consider it a sheer gift, friends, when tests and challenges come at you from all sides. You know that under pressure, your faith-life is forced into the open and shows its true colors. So don't try to get out of anything prematurely. Let it do its work so you become mature and well-developed, not deficient in any way. (James 1:2–4 MSG)

Don't confuse trials in life with failures, weaknesses, or bad thinking like, "I'm not tall enough, old enough, strong enough, smart enough, bold enough, etc." And don't mix it with people who don't like you. You will *never* get that concrete hardened with components like these in the mix.

We have all heard of people who have suffered greatly in life then turned and ministered health and healing to those going through the exact thing. But one cannot do that until they're strengthened and made whole from God Himself.

People in this day and age are coasting. They say that they pray. They go to church. They know some Bible verses. But their real absolute is, "Anything goes." They're like a chameleon. They fit in everywhere.

Living life in the zone is imperative.

> "Everyone who hears my words and obeys them is like a wise man who built his house on rock. It rained hard, the floods came, and the winds blew and hit that house. But it did not fall, because it was built on rock. Everyone who hears my

> words and does not obey them is like a foolish man who built his house on sand. It rained hard, the floods came, and the winds blew and hit that house, and it fell with a big crash." (Matt. 7:24–27 NCV)

Absolutes take your sand and make it concrete: a sure foundation with no shifting. Jesus's seed was set. Check out E. W. Kenyon's *The Redemption of Man*. You'll understand the whole plot, as God wrote it in His book.

> The scroll of Isaiah the prophet was handed to him. He unrolled the scroll and found the place where this was written: "The Spirit of the Lord is upon me, for he has anointed me to bring Good News to the poor.
>
> "He has sent me to proclaim that captives will be released, that the blind will see, that the oppressed will be set free, and that the time of the Lord's favor has come." (Luke 4:17–19 NLT)

He knew exactly who He was and why He was here. That gave Him the story line for every chapter contained in the book of His everyday life. Oh, He had plenty of antagonists in His story, but His life's direction was set and He did not allow any vacillation from it. How would your life's story read? What would be the title of the book about your life? What have you to say to others to help them in their lives?

The ditches are filled with drifted seeds, right next to focused fields. It doesn't mean they're not pretty, but they're almost impossible to harvest. Ditches aren't generally harvested, and fields aren't generally discarded. Life is about finishing. It's about production and harvest. Life is about the full corn in the ear. Mingled seed and drifting lives don't reach full "harvestability."

A *fact* is a description of the present state of a thing. But don't judge everything by the facts. Facts are *always* subject to change. Are you older in life as you read this book about change? That doesn't matter. Most successful people accomplish their "full corn in the ear" after the age of sixty. It takes spring and summer, after all, to grow a plant so that it can produce fruit to be harvested in the fall.

God puts everything on the inside. All God created has the potential principle inside it. Remember that He says He looks at the heart, not on the outward appearance.

> People judge by outward appearance, but the Lord looks at the heart. (1 Sam. 16:7c NLT)
>
> You have been regenerated (born again), not from a mortal origin (seed, sperm), but from one that is immortal by the ever living and lasting Word of God. (1 Pet. 1:23 AMPC)

It's His seed in you. You must get it started, give it the right conditions to grow. God loves the sinner because of what He has put on the inside of him. He can get it out of you if you'll cooperate with Him. God has ways no man can even think of. He puts the finish in the start. He sees the end of a thing, and *then* He begins. This is why faith is actually easy! God thinks this way: calling things that be not as though they *already are* (Rom. 4:17). So should we. Be a visionary of what your particular seed could produce.

You know what a chair is. You can picture it in your mind, right? If everyone drew a picture of a chair, they may be different in looks but identifiable by their purpose. Their purpose is to keep you from having to sit on the floor. What if you were as sure of the Word of God as you are when you see a chair and know it's a chair? What if you just started believing the Word and stopped questioning whether it's true for you? Whether it really works? Whether God loves you? Because when you believe, the kind of faith Jesus talks about is easy. And this is what pleases God, after all. He just wants to be believed. Don't you? When you know something is true and someone contests it, don't you just want to be believed? So does God. Change your own list of absolutes to agree with God.

> But without faith it is impossible to please him: for he that cometh to God must believe that He is, and that he is a rewarder of them that diligently seek him. (Heb. 11:6 KJV)

18

Weeds in the Soil

Weeds are the easiest things to grow. They're formed by implementation of this common expression: Que será, será. Whatever will be, will be. The horticultural definition of a *weed* is "any plant that is out of place." Therefore, even a sweet-smelling rose is considered a weed if it's standing tall and beautiful in the wrong place.

Sometimes weeds may seem acceptable. They are unrecognizable as a weed, like that rose. We've already covered how people can negatively influence your focus even if they're well-meaning, sweet-smelling, rose-petaled associates like G. W. Carver's lab technicians. Carver loved and cared about his associates (protégées), but when it came to God speaking to him, he allowed no distractions.

Weeds can hide, that's for sure. Let's say, for example, that you have a generous uncle who cares about you and keeps up on what's happening in your life. Perhaps he even put you through college. If he's void of Christian values, his advice and influence in your life should be accessed with great caution.

You end up with a big mess if you allow weeds. They're the greatest thieves, stealing your spot in the field of life. They take the nutrients, water, and in actuality, the place meant for you. Weeds ultimately steal your fruit, as a plant engulfed by weeds will never come to the fruit stage in life. Stress can be a weed. Fruit is the first thing to be sacrificed by a plant under stress. That's why doctors advise women who can't conceive to just relax. That's why wise CEOs make sure their top dogs get vacations, so that when they return from time off, their ideas will be fresh. Fruit. That's the goal.

> Every branch in me that beareth not fruit he taketh away: and every branch that beareth fruit, he purgeth it, that it may bring forth more fruit. (John 15:2 KJV)

God purges what's in your life that doesn't produce, but you must also examine yourself and take action before the Holy Spirit has to inform you of the necessary change. Not only can people be weeds, but of course, so can thoughts. Analyze your thinking and be on the lookout for weeds. You have to cull out and cultivate from time to time.

> You have not chosen Me, but I have chosen you and I have appointed you [I have planted you], that you might go and bear fruit *and* keep on bearing, and that your fruit may be lasting [that it may remain, abide], so that whatever you ask the Father in My Name [as presenting all that I Am], He may give it to you. (John 15:16 AMPC)

Even Jesus had to set family aside in order to focus on what was before Him.

> Someone told Jesus, "Your mother and your brothers are standing outside, and they want to speak to you."
>
> Jesus asked, "Who is my mother? Who are my brothers?" Then he pointed to his disciples and said, "Look, these are my mother and brothers. Anyone who does the will of my Father in heaven is my brother and sister and mother!" (Matt. 12:47–50 NLT)

Abram was told to leave his home and family in order to fulfill the purpose God had for him in his life, which essentially was to begin the Jewish nation. Unfortunately, Abram didn't heed God's Word to the letter and took along his nephew Lot, who became an ongoing problem for him (Genesis 12). Sometimes things look exactly like what you want but, under close scrutiny, are found out to be weed-infested. For example, darnel is a weed that looks just like wheat.

Weeds, as well as insects and grubs, are a real nuisance. We may think weeds are a seasonal thing, but they can be a daily, if not minute-by-minute, problem for people. Planting your crop is seasonal, but that is not how weeds play the game. When you cultivate your crop, weeds pop back up within the week. They are relentless. You need weed killer. The greatest weed killer is a scripture we've presented before. The following box contains the Message Bible version.

> Summing it all up, friends, I'd say you'll do best by filling your minds and med-

> itating on things true, noble, reputable, authentic, compelling, gracious—the best, not the worst; the beautiful, not the ugly; things to praise, not things to curse. Put into practice what you learned from me, what you heard and saw and realized. Do that, and God, who makes everything work together, will work you into his most excellent harmonies. (Phil. 4:8–9 MSG)

You don't just stop thinking a thought—you have to replace it with another. Remember Luke 11:24–26? The demon comes back to find the previous place he occupied has been clean and swept, but nothing has taken its place. He therefore takes over worse than before. After all, there's nothing there to prevent him.

Weeds want to pollinate. Wrong theories, thoughts, and words want to pollinate and reproduce to overtake the field. They're aggressive, and it will require work to dispose of them. They sometimes have strong roots. You cannot allow them to grow as big as a tree.

Here's the quirk of it all. The more you let them grow, the more you seem to be accepted by family and friends. They think you're okay. When you go to work to change the inner you, you become the Jesus freak, the Bible-thumper, or the holier-than-thou dude. What is it about family and friends who just don't want us to improve ourselves? They are only interested in forming you into their expectations. Sometimes they're not comfortable with change in any form. They want to hold you in your old self.

Weeds easily arise from a life lived by accepting the unprofitable words and unproductive methods of generations past. A person's soil condition exists, and weeds can be present long before you arrive. Who were your parents, grandparents, and even great-grandparents? What were their habits? How did they handle stress and pressure? What did you witness as a young plant growing up? Sometimes the acorn doesn't fall far from the tree. You're just a chip off the old block. Or are you? In what part of the world were you born? What was the environment? Culture? Conditions? All this has a part to play in who you are and what you think and believe to be the truth. All this plays a part in the weeds you allow to grow and/or the fruit you produce. Do you have some of those handsome roses present in your personal patch? Are there weeds in your family who don't approve of God's calling in your life?

On the flip side, there is a discernment that comes with growth and years. You didn't arrive at this place in your life on your own. If at any time you slow down and ponder your life, you realize that you came from somewhere. You could say one hundred things about one hundred people in your life so far. So many have added good things to your soil condition. Sometimes you've learned more from your enemies than from your friends. Remember that soil is the heart, your core, the inner you. It's so important to pluck out any weeds growing there.

The nice thing is, soil can be changed. Weeds can be pulled. Additives can be cultivated into your soil to bring levels of deficiencies up. Does the pH show too much acid? Add some lime. Is there too much depression in your life? As we've already learned, add the speaking and believing of what God thinks of you and stop saying what *you* think of you and what you've been taught.

All you have to do in your life to produce weeds is to go idle. They'll come up immediately without planting. They were waiting there to germinate. If you want weeds to grow, just allow every random thought. Just meditate on all your past problems—let them percolate in the coffeepot of your mind. Then start voicing all the negative things you're thinking. Make the picture complete by hanging your head in dejection directly afterward.

> A tree is identified by its fruit. If a tree is good, its fruit will be good. If a tree is bad, its fruit will be bad. You brood of snakes! How could evil men like you speak what is good and right? For whatever is in your heart determines what you say. A good person produces good things from the treasury of a good heart, and an evil person produces evil things from the treasury of an evil heart. (Matt. 12:33–35 NLT)

Repair the damage and bring in nutrients. Call those things that be not as though they are, and soon they will be! The potter forms the clay. You form your life in so many ways, on purpose. And if you allow it, other faith-filled folks can speak wisdom into your life. The Word of God is used for correction.

> Since you were a child you have known the Holy Scriptures which are able to

> make you wise. And that wisdom leads to salvation through faith in Christ Jesus. All Scripture is inspired by God and is useful for teaching, for showing people what is wrong in their lives, for correcting faults, and for teaching how to live right. Using the Scriptures, the person who serves God will be capable, having all that is needed to do every good work. (2 Tim. 3:15–17 NCV)

While in the weed chapter, I might as well tell a weed story. My brother did some drastic changing of his soil. He spent some time pulling weeds. He ran away from home at the age of seventeen and traveled out West to get away from the wrong things he experienced from family and surroundings as a youth. Now, looking back, he has managed to take the best of both parents. He displays a calm, faith-filled demeanor like our mother, and he adopted the intelligent business mind of our father. (I did, too, but then I'm the one writing this book!) Although he might not have been supported in his younger years and had to redirect his thought life as a result, he did overcome and has become successful in life. He did this through faith.

He made the choice as a young man to accept Jesus as his Savior and head in the opposite way he was drifting. Almost instantly, that choice was challenged. He had been dabbling in drugs and alcohol as a teenager. One day, he made that commitment to Jesus. A week after that decision, he found a bag of drugs lying on the ground as he walked along. His first thought? "Wow. What a boon!" He picked up the bag and recognized that it was some good stuff. His second thought was, "If only I had found this a week ago. I don't do this anymore. It will take me back in the wrong direction." With the two deliberations waging war in his mind, the final question came up: "What should I do?"

Temptation had come. The test was on. He said, "Jesus, I've only known You a couple of days, but I would rather walk with You not knowing exactly where I'm headed than to smoke this and know where it will take me." He chose the new road. I'll give you one guess as to what he did next. He dumped the contents of the bag on the ground, watched it blow away in the breeze, and kept walking.

There was that untamed kitten again. Can God trust him? And will he trust God? Can he trust that the new life he chose would indeed bring the sought-after change he was desperate for? He made the choice right then and has never strayed from that decision to "just say no" to drug use.

There are two ways we learn in life: before the problem occurs or after. In your thinking, clarity is the opposite of confusion. When you make and speak out the decisions for your life *before* the test, you'll find your route much easier. You practice this on a clear day when there are no problems. You say, "I will not commit adultery. I will not steal. I will not do drugs. I will not _____." You make that choice so that when the pressure comes, your decision has already been made. It's almost like you're creating your own road signs for direction on the freeway of life you'll be traveling tomorrow. You must be able to pull in all the words that support a clear view. In that way, you make strong pathways in your brain. Read one of the brain books listed in the "Recommended Reading" section of this book to find out what goes on in the mind pathologically and electrically when you make a decision. You can't think of two things at the same time, so the one pushes the other out. That's how it works. That's how you do this:

> For the weapons of our warfare are not physical [weapons of flesh and blood], but they are mighty before God for the overthrow and destruction of strongholds, [inasmuch as we] refute arguments and theories and reasonings and every proud and lofty thing that sets itself up against the [true] knowledge of God; and we lead every thought and purpose away captive into the obedience of Christ (the Messiah, the Anointed One). (2 Cor. 10:4–5 AMPC)

When you do this, you're mulching your soil. You're protecting it against weeds and other plants wanting to take over and grow.

As long as you're still breathing in air, the end of your story has not been written, and you have the potential to change your future. You're never too old to become what you might be. Water yourself daily. It's about the fruit you were destined to produce, for someone else. You'll find that self-centeredness must leave. And you must ask God what *He* wants. No seed can enter a hardened heart. Conversely, the seed must relinquish all its rights unconditionally to the soil. Humility is when a seed humbles itself and submits. It discovers its potential and doesn't argue with the soil. The only guarantee is that things will change.

As a young believer, I attended church. I gave reluctantly. But as I allowed the Word to go deep into my soil, I realized my motivation in giving was incorrect. As I began to tithe, I did it out of obedience to what I read in the Word, but I didn't necessarily like it. I had a lot of places I wanted that money to go, and church wasn't one of them. I did not have a cheery heart in my giving. I was obedient but not willing.

> Each one must do as he has made up his mind, not reluctantly or under compulsion, for God loves a cheerful giver. (2 Cor. 9:7 RSV)

As I studied God's character, I discovered His heart as a giver. He truly freely gives. *Yes,* I conceded within my thoughts, *I want to become more like Him.* With that, I discovered that He wasn't trying to get something from me but rather to give something *to* me, as you see in the verses both before and after this paragraph.

> The point is this: he who sows sparingly will also reap sparingly, and he who sows bountifully will also reap bountifully.
>
> And God is able to provide you with every blessing in abundance, so that you may always have enough of everything and may provide in abundance for every good work. (2 Cor. 9:6, 8 RSV)

Now as I freely give, I realize God broke that covetous attitude of "me first." God knows He can trust that I won't put money above Him. And I've overcome the fear of not having enough.

We have now arrived at what I believe to be the greatest weed grown and allowed: fear. Every person deals with it at some level. God is adamantly against you allowing fear in any form. It's the main tool of the enemy. If he can stop you because of your fears, he's won.

There are hundreds of known and classified phobias and plenty of weird ones never yet identified as such. People won't get on a plane because of the fear of death. They call it all kinds of names, like being cautious. People won't tithe or give because of the fear of lack. They call it being frugal, but it's stinginess. These are the weeds we allow. In fact, we think they're flowers! They're the fruit. We tell ourselves lies about the fears we have so we won't have to face them.

Overcome your fears. In order to pull weeds, you sometimes have to speak out the opposite of what seems real. Don't speak every problem, worry, and doubt that you have. The common acronym used for FEAR is "false evidence appearing real." How do we develop great soil? Water it with the Word of God and weed it often. Perfect love with trust in the Father will take care of any fear. Memorize Psalm 27. Read Psalm 91 every day. That will settle the issue of fear for you.

> There is no room in love for fear. Well-formed love banishes fear. Since fear is crippling, a fearful life—fear of death, fear of judgment—is one not yet fully formed in love. (1 John 4:18 MSG)

19

Soil: The Dirty Little Secret

My and my wife's soils instructor in college would cringe at this chapter's title. It's just a pun on words. It's not a secret at all. And it's not dirty. The professor's definition of *soil* was "a plant-growing medium." His definition of *dirt* was "what's under your fingernails." We were never allowed to call our plant-growing medium dirt in class.

The professor's definition is exactly correct. In God's eyes, soil *is* the growing medium for planted seed, but He calls it "the heart" or "the inner man" of the heart. So if soil represents the heart in the Bible, every time you see the word *soil* in the Word, you can substitute the word *heart*. And then when you read the word, think in terms of *your* heart, your core, and your inner man.

> That he would grant you, according to the riches of his glory, to be strengthened with might by his Spirit in the inner man;
>
> That Christ may dwell in your hearts by faith; that ye, being rooted and grounded in love,
>
> May be able to comprehend with all saints what is the breadth, and length, and depth, and height;
>
> And to know the love of Christ, which passeth knowledge, that ye might

> be filled with all the fulness of God. (Eph. 3:16–19 KJV)

Soil is the proving ground of life. Everything gets filtered through the soil. That is why God says He looks at the heart. Jesus taught from the Word directly to the heart of those who would listen with a spiritual ear alert to understand.

Do you know the parable that Jesus considered the most important for which to grasp the meaning? It's the parable that unlocks the door to all the parables that He used to explain God's purpose and plan and how to live in the zone.

> Then Jesus said to them, "If you can't understand the meaning of this parable, how will you understand all the other parables?" (Mark 4:13 NLT)

I'd say that's a pretty good highlight on the parable of the sower. I'll go into this all-important allegory Jesus taught later in this chapter.

First, it's important to understand that soil is the most important component for growing a seed. It's the *source*, or conduit, for everything the plant takes in. Soil has the ability to retain moisture or to lose it. A good field can take up to six inches of rain. Bad soil (termed hardpan) is able to absorb nothing, nada, nil, naught, zero, zilch, zippo before the droplets start to run off. Make sure that's not you! Don't be hardpan.

Soil is used to provide nutrients to a tree, to make strong, healthy leaves, and to hold that tree in place when tempest winds try to blow it over. It's like your home. You sleep there, eat there, and live there. How well fortified and cared for do you keep your home?

Soil will try to grow anything. You can plant a seed or a spoon, and that soil will do its job of trying to break down any outer shell to release the inner root and shoot. Earth is amazing. It's programmed by the Creator. It does what it's supposed to do.

> And He (Jesus) said, "So is the kingdom of God, as if a man should cast seed into the ground; and should sleep, and rise night and day, and the seed should spring and grow up, he knoweth not how. For

> the earth bringeth forth fruit of herself."
> (Mark 4:26–28a KJV)

We have a thirty-five-year-old flowering hibiscus. The base of the trunk is huge. It blooms beautifully all season: five-inch bright-red double blossoms! On occasion, to curb and correct its ubiquitous growth, we cut it back until there is nothing green left. A few months later, it's bigger and better than before. If we fail to fortify the soil (fertilize) in the spring before we transfer it outside, we'll experience wilted, sunburned leaves, dropped buds, and a long recovery time. I think you already know where I'm going with this narrative.

Bad soil equals a weak tree. It's susceptible to virus, parasites, woodpeckers, and falling down altogether. Similarly, the body's heart is the pumping station for the lifeblood to flow. A bad heart equals a weak body. Our heart (inner man) can be susceptible to deviant thinking, corrupt doctrine, bad companions, and wrong decision-making if it's not fortified. Ultimately, a person will end up making a poor decision, sometimes so bad he will be unable to return to the place from where he started.

With our hibiscus, enriched soil makes the leaves hearty and strong to withstand full summer sun, wind, and pounding rain. If we remember to fertilize it, we enjoy the fruits of our labor all season. It's amazing and foolproof. It's a law of nature. If we're lazy about it, we reap the results of frail, thin, wispy leaves that are light green in color. The comparison here? You must regularly strengthen your heart with Bible-rich sustenance. It's crucial, absolutely crucial. Remember, the goal is to flower. The finish is to have fruit, and that the fruit would remain and not drop before harvesttime. Be the self-corrector. Cut back whatever weak and spindly growth you have so that proper, pure-direction growth can take the lead. You never really know what's ahead in your life. You'd do well to be ready when troubles come.

> If you faint in the day of adversity, thy strength is weak. (Prov. 24:10 KJV)

The fool says, "I'm going to the bar." The wise man says, "I'm going to sit quietly for one hour and see what God says to me." Every minute, you're making choices. You become what you have decided. It creates a rhythm. What's yours? Purpose has a supernatural ability to order your steps, to blow into your sails. Your desire dictates your behavior. Doesn't it? The intensity of your desire determines your level of effect within that behavior. The banks of your river narrow with intensity.

So let's look closely at the parable Jesus identified as the gatekeeper to understanding all others.

> "Listen! A farmer went out to plant some seed. As he scattered it across his field, some of the seed fell on a footpath, and the birds came and ate it. Other seed fell on shallow soil with underlying rock. The seed sprouted quickly because the soil was shallow. But the plant soon wilted under the hot sun, and since it didn't have deep roots, it died. Other seed fell among thorns that grew up and choked out the tender plants so they produced

> no grain. Still other seeds fell on fertile soil, and they sprouted, grew, and produced a crop that was thirty, sixty, and even a hundred times as much as had been planted!" Then he said, "Anyone with ears to hear should listen and understand." (Mark 4:3–8 NLT)

This passage says that there are four types of soil, but only one is rich and good for long-term growth. Life is a long hike, not a jaunt to the mailbox. Anybody can be a flash in the pan, but get your back up against the wall and you find out what you really believe and of what your soil is composed, or "compost," to engage another pun on words.

The one who is actively biblically engaged in their own life is the one who has a compost pile at their endless disposal. A compost pile is a valuable asset when maintaining a healthy garden. Remember Olga's garden? She used to speak of the decaying compost as if it were the very life-giver to her dazzling hobby. She would have the farmer from down the road add a batch of his precious manure to her garden from time to time. She spoke of it as if it were gold—its qualities, consistency, and yes, even its rich smell. Olga would then laugh as she caught herself and remembered what it was she was speaking so highly of.

Compost has a concentrated collection of rich nutrients. When you repeat and believe Scripture, it's like possessing a compost pile. These positive words that you're now well-seasoned in saying to yourself (or about that negative situation) will come back and cause you to bloom, bright and beautiful, whereas others would collapse in despair. Hang around a negative naysayer and you can almost smell the stench. Hang around an up-talker and you can tell the goodness they feed on. The aroma from their speech is pleasant to the nostrils *and* the ears. It's like a blood transfusion to a weak, sickly, anemic person.

When troubles come, what do you speak from your heart? Doubt? Anger? Depression? Do you have rich soil or depleted, spent, drained, and dry soil? Remember that seeds in the ground are words that are planted in our hearts, according to Jesus's definition to His disciples later in chapter 4 of Mark. Hear what he says:

> The farmer plants seed by taking God's Word to others. The seed that fell on the footpath represents those who hear the message, only to have Satan come at once and take it away. The seed on the rocky soil represents those who hear the message and immediately receive it with joy. But since they don't have deep roots, they don't last long. They fall away as soon as they have problems or are persecuted for believing God's word. The seed that fell among the thorns represents others who hear God's word, but all too quickly the message is crowded out by the worries of this life, the lure of wealth, and the desire for other things, so no fruit is produced. And the seed that fell on good soil represents those who hear and accept God's word and produce a harvest of thirty, sixty, or even a hundred times as much as had been planted!" (Mark 4:14–20 NLT)

Do you have wayside seeds still hanging out in your heart? Have they fallen on hardpan? Words that you heard but weren't ready to believe? They flit in and flit out and take no root, because you just can't "buy it"?

It's interesting that the Greek word for *devil* is *diabolos*. Its translation isn't what you think. It means "to throw like a rock." Satan works on our minds and throws thoughts at us, like, "That's hogwash! Don't believe that lie!"

Genesis 3:5 contains the lie of all lies. Satan convinced Eve (and Adam was right there with her), saying, "You will be like God, knowing good from evil." What a great deal! To be more like God is desirable. Eve was after the right thing but through the wrong means. She knew what God had said about that particular tree in the garden. My question is, What were they doing hanging around it? (They were definitely coming against one of the absolutes found in Proverbs and in Psalm 1. There's a lesson to be learned there.) But she fell for the lie. I can't think of a better time for the husband to step in with some discernment than at that moment when his wife is being lied to by God's enemy. Adam had been told (in the literal Hebrew) that "in dying, thou shalt die." Adam's body died later, but his tight relationship with the Father died immediately. They lost the open door to God's presence. They lost the privilege of living life in the zone. It's Jesus who has regained it for us. Now He is the open door, and the *only* one at that.

> Jesus told him, "I am the way, the truth, and the life. No one can come to the Father except through me." (John 14:6 NLT)

The stony soil is the short-term believer. He loves what he hears and responds well to it, but under life's pressures, he abandons it altogether. These folks never make the connection between what they hear, what they act on, and what they allow to go deep into their hearts. It's like sugar-candied gum—sweet at the start, but the gum inside gets stale and old after a bit of chewing. It gets spit out.

The third kind of soil allows all the wonderful, beautiful bounty of this life to overtake the wealth of the treasure of the Word. Pretty soon the question is asked, "God who? Oh yeah, I remember that God phase I went through in college." God gave us all things richly to enjoy but never to take the place of thrilling our hearts more than God Himself. Enjoy Him. A relationship with Him is much more fulfilling than earthly riches. He so loves to give. But get priorities out of whack and the spigot will close.

> Teach those who are rich in this world not to be proud and not to trust in their money, which is so unreliable. Their trust should be in God, who richly gives us all we need for our enjoyment. Tell them to use their money to do good. They should be rich in good works and generous to those in need, always being ready to share with others. By doing this they will be storing up their treasure as a good foundation for the future so that they may experience true life. (1 Tim. 6:17–19 NLT)

Have worldly things left you feeling dry? Then you're at the place where God can fully enrich your soil and excite you in a way that the world never could. Are you reading all the Scripture boxes in this book? Or are you skipping over them because "you know that already"? Every time you read even one scripture, you inject your soil with a dose of fertilizer. The only difference in the comparison is that, spiritually speaking, you can't overfertilize your soil. You're reinforcing that connection in your brain. Your spirit-man says, "Yes, I agree with that scripture." You refamiliarize yourself with it until it's like tying your shoe for the millionth time.

I have to echo the Word to myself constantly. I never know when I might need some truth, and if it's not readily there in a well-worn pathway, I can't draw from it. Someone once said, "I have to keep filling myself up with the Word because I leak." Yes, we do forget things. That's why living in the zone is the key. It keeps distractions like the third kind of soil at bay.

I remember doing a job once in Kentucky. We were to load a semi by hand with valuable, resalable goods, and *none* of my scheduled workers showed up, not a single one. Why? Kentucky doesn't generally get very cold, and we all woke up to a bitterly cold wind with subfreezing temps. Covington natives weren't used to this. My prospective workers must have decided that, for the wage per hour, they were not prepared to endure this hardship. They must have decided to hunker down for the day, as not one person answered my phone call.

I was in desperate shape. The empty fifty-three-foot truck was on its way, and not one piece of furniture was staged in the parking lot, ready to load. But God was about to show Himself strong on my behalf. It puts a smile on my face to remember the event. I choose to remember the fruit of it, not the stress of it.

I had tilled my soil that morning and had planted some great seeds of faith. I always do, especially when I'm about to tackle a big job. I had spoken out loud my trust in Him before my feet hit the floor that morning.

An onlooker might have thought I was worrying while I paced the hotel lobby floor, but in truth, I was waiting on God. I called on God for a plan B, if happily He might have one. As I communed with Him, I heard Him tell me to go across the street to McDonald's. I said, "God, I don't need a cup of coffee. I need workers." Nonetheless, at that familiar voice to my spirit, I followed His lead. I tucked my ears down under my collar and walked over to the fast-food restaurant. When I entered, my eye caught several men—older, homeless men—hunkering down themselves in the restaurant. I gathered by the caps they wore that they were Vietnam veterans. I ordered coffee and asked the cashier about them. She said they were welcomed to come in and warm up on cold days.

Aha! I knew immediately why the coffee suggestion from God. I had the answer to my petition. I pointed to each vet individually and asked if they wanted to earn some cash that day. They looked at one another, shrugged, and each, in turn, nodded in agreement.

Those homeless war veterans were the best workers I ever hired! They were respectful, appreciative, and anxious to do a good job for me. They worked hard in the cold all day, and I rewarded each one with a bonus. When I had left the McDonald's with the men in tow, the employees applauded for me, and for them. It was a win-win-win situation God invited me to partake in. He had it planned the entire time. I just needed to tune out the distractions (like my distress) and get into the zone. I needed to be calm and enter into His rest so that I could hear His voice.

> Dear brothers and sisters, when troubles of any kind come your way, consider it an opportunity for great joy. For you know that when your faith is tested, your endurance has a chance to grow. So let it grow, for when your endurance is fully developed, you will be perfect and complete, needing nothing. (James 1:2–4 NLT)

At this point in my life, trials are not what they used to be. Now I look at them like large building blocks to step onto, leading to a new, higher platform. I've seen God do some amazing things—things not easily forgotten. I view many situations in life just like David viewed Goliath. David was more incensed at this fellow standing against God than anything else. But it wasn't David's fight. It was God's.

So are *all* our fights and trials in life. They're God's. Let Him fight for you. He's your dad. Permit Him to make a way when there seems to be no way. Your job is to form first-rate, rich soil with which to receive and birth forth seed.

> But the seed planted in the good earth represents those who hear the Word, embrace it, and produce a harvest beyond their wildest dreams. (Mark 4:20 MSG)

20
Soil Condition: Vital to Growth

Ruling Israel, David was God's man for the task. King Saul was chosen by the people because of his stature and kingly appearance, but he didn't have God's heart. His power and position went to his head. That inroad stroked his ego like a hand on soft puppy ears. You can read about him in 1 Samuel, but it's David's heart I want to unveil.

He was usually found in his father's pastures, watching the sheep, where he spent many an hour building a relationship and communing with God. I believe David was very practiced at living in the zone. You can't write that many emotion-moving, faith-filled songs (Psalms) without being highly in tune with the Holy Spirit. He kept his soil in exceptional condition. He also had his fair share of trials in life. His life story is a good example when it comes to what I'm writing about in this book, living in (and/or out of) the zone.

David's coming of full spiritual stature happened when he was a young teenager. Bible scholars' best guess is that he was about fourteen or fifteen years old at the time he met up with Goliath. For David, this gargantuan hulk was just another lion or bear, a threat coming against what he valued in life and whom he would get the victory over. But for forty thousand other men, this was a tremendous trial, one that left them shaking in their boots. They were hiding out and unwilling to face the fear, the Bible says. That bears witness with my spirit that this is a common malady with people: an unwillingness to face our own fears.

> As soon as the Israelite army saw him, they began to run away in fright. "Have you seen the giant?" the men asked. "He comes out each day to defy Israel. The king has offered a huge reward to anyone who kills him. He will give that man one of his daughters for a wife, and the man's entire family will be exempted from paying taxes!" David asked the soldiers standing nearby, "What will a man get for killing this Philistine and ending his defiance of Israel? Who is this pagan Philistine anyway, that he is allowed to defy the armies of the living God?" (1 Sam. 17:24–26 NLT)

I believe it was all a setup from God. Out of that many men, there could not be found a Navy SEAL type for the job? This taunting from their enemy went on for a month. Talk about dragging out the fear! Perfect timing for the Father to bring out His pint-size, God-seeking prayer warrior David to enter the scene and show off the power of the God of Israel.

For David, this was just an opportunity to move forward and take a step up. How do I know that? Didn't he ask what the prize would be for the one who would conquer the giant? In fact, according to some Bible versions, he asked twice just to make sure of his upcoming reward. That shows a man, young as he may be, not considering defeat as an option. It shows David was confident in His God and ready for promotion. It shows a man who thought the way God thought, seeing the end from the beginning. He saw himself with his foot on the monster's head while he cut it off with the enemy's own huge sword. What a foolish enemy to mess with the famed God of Israel. And from the account of the true tale, David carried that head around with him like a trophy for a good long while, showing off God's and his victory. He earned it, after all.

> David took the Philistine's head to Jerusalem, but he stored the man's armor in his own tent. (1 Sam. 17:54 NLT)
>
> As soon as David returned from killing Goliath, Abner brought him to Saul with the Philistine's head still in his hand. (1 Sam. 17:57 NLT)

What gave David the ability to kill Goliath? Was he bigger? Certainly not. Smarter? No. Wealthier? No. Was he an experienced warrior in hand-to-hand combat? Nope. What was different about David was that his soil was fortified from all the quiet time he spent with God. He knew that he knew that he knew that he knew that God was for him! You see, the forty thousand men were comparing the giant to themselves and their abilities, whereas David was comparing the giant to God and His abilities.

> What then shall we say to [all] this? If God is for us, who [can be] against us? [Who can be our foe, if God is on our side?]. (Rom. 8:31 AMPC)

This is seeing the end before it begins. It's God's method. The presence and subsequent power of God in your life: there's nothing like it. When you get into a tough spot, it's not the time to tuck tail and run. It's the time to stand tall and say, "Oh! An advancement has arrived." Reassess. Start speaking to yourself. Reach out, because tough spots cause you to reach. That's what roots do—they reach. They stretch. They can push through concrete or rock when necessary.

Push through to find areas in your life you never knew existed. Then what was once a thought, a dream, and a subsequent goal is now a platform from which to reach again. This event demonstrates a principle that exists in your life every day, every minute. Whether it's your marriage, your finances, your job, or whatever other arena from which a challenge may arise, the Word from God states that you can do *anything* when put your trust in Him.

> I have strength for all things in Christ Who empowers me [I am ready for anything and equal to anything through Him Who infuses inner strength into me; I am self-sufficient in Christ's sufficiency]. (Phil. 4:13 AMPC)

This clearly gives you more than an edge to win. God did not send Jesus to die for you so that you would fail.

A baby gets spoon-fed. Then as that baby grows, he has to reach for Cheerios on the tray. Then he sits at the table and has to put a sandwich to his mouth. Then he has to walk to the kitchen and make his own sandwich. Then he has to get a job, go to the grocery store and buy the ingredients to make the sandwich. Such is the sequence of growth. Growth causes you to take steps that ultimately cause you to run the race. Remember, the narrow road is a road under pressure. Don't cringe at the challenge; just recognize it for what it is: a growth spurt.

A tree that endures drought or flooding, forceful winds, or scorching, relentless sun day after day just sends out deeper roots to secure it. When you look at nature, it's absolutely amazing what plants have been able to come through and survive quite nicely. They have setbacks in growth, yes, but they survive and sometimes thrive. Remember looking at a slice of tree trunk in school and counting the rings to figure the age of the tree? Some rings are narrow, indicating a troubled year of growth, and some rings are wide, indicating ease. So it is with our lives. Jesus said rain falls on us all alike (Matt. 5:45).

Here's a perfect example of this challenge-meeting principle from a friend's life. I'll call her Linda. She had a sweet, innocent, intelligent, articulate daughter whom I'll call Lisa. In third grade, Lisa encountered a teacher who didn't like her. The recommendation from friends to the mother was that she pull her daughter out and put her in the other third-grade class with a nicer teacher. Linda wouldn't do it. She said, "My daughter needs to learn the lesson in life that not everyone is going to like her. She needs to learn how to deal with that. She needs to find out and put out what this teacher demands of her."

The good parent is the one who does not pave the way for their child but allows trials to build character. The good parent is the one who prepares the child for that day when they are old enough to be on their own, sure of themselves from practice, confident in their abilities, knowing their weaknesses yet excited to make their imprint on the world.

The good parent is the one who teaches them real life and how to be successful overcomers, not protecting them from every stumbling block that comes across their path. In this way, they disable negative experiences and turn them into victories that fortify the soil of the young child. All the while the parent is turning their child toward God, in essence placing their child's hand in the hand of Jesus. They're showing them how to put their trust in the only one truly able to protect them wherever they go and whatever they do in life. A fearful parent is a dangerous one, dangerous to that child's safety and well-being.

> Don't you realize that in a race everyone runs, but only one person gets the prize? So run to win! All athletes are disciplined in their training. They do it to win a prize that will fade away, but we do it for an eternal prize. So I run with purpose in every step. I am not just shadowboxing. I discipline my body like an athlete, training it to do what it should. Otherwise, I fear that after preaching to others I myself might be disqualified. (1 Cor. 9:24–27 NLT)

Make no mistake: trials play a very important part in a healthy life, so how you view them is vital. Maybe in heaven life is perfect and there is no need for growth and development, but here on earth, not facing your own contests is not good for you. These tests are different for every individual, and you can't take the test for another person. It's designed for you. It's got the composition necessary for *your* soil and *your* personal growth. Don't set yourself up for trouble down the road, like having a quitter's mentality, to name one. We're all familiar with the feeling of failure. It's not pretty. And it's definitely not in God's plan for you. Lisa, by the way, turned out to be one confident woman, obtaining a college degree in a tough field of study.

I was a wrestler in high school. Remember, I was an angry young man at that time. I think back now, and I feel sorry for my opponents, whoever they might have been. From the time we were getting ready in the locker room until we were weighing in and then sitting by the mat, waiting our turn, I was working the guy. I was messing with his mind. At all times, I stared him down with a glare that said, "I'm going to tear you apart on that mat!" Every time he would look my way, I'm sure he said to himself, "What's with this guy? Is he crazy?" You see, most guys who went out for sports did it for a different reason than I did. Engaging in sports allowed me the place to vent so that I *wouldn't* vent my anger on someone in the wrong way. That made me a fierce competitor. My coaches always liked me because they recognized there was no "quit" in me. You know the deal. I won matches for them and for the team. All coaches like that. The wrestler who beat me in my junior year took state. In my life, I never got rid of that victor's mindset, but it's reserved for a different contender now. I battle the devil, and I discipline my thinking. In the end, he never wins. I'm the winner!

The main battle and one of the first battles you'll ever fight is the battle within yourself. Lurking inside each one of us are weak spots, cracks in our foundation, and tendencies to give up. How you win over these areas is up to you, but win you must. You'll never beat the devil if you don't change your own soil. If you do manage to change your soil, every good seed will come looking for you because it will find a great place to grow. Seeds are opportunities to grow more like God. One day you'll look back and say, "How did all this happen?" It seems to me that God always blesses in seed form. Seeds germinate, and fruit comes. Blessings grow in the believer's life when they are doers of the Word.

Life is about transformation, and that never stops. Whatever your trials (and we all have them), face them being sure of God's backing in your life. I'll say it again. He loves you. He longs to be the one for you to go to for help with whatever the fear or trial.

> Take [with me] your share of the hardships and suffering [which you are called to endure] as a good (first-class) soldier of Christ Jesus.
>
> No soldier when in service gets entangled in the enterprises of [civilian] life; his aim is to satisfy and please the one who enlisted him.
>
> And if anyone enters competitive games, he is not crowned unless he competes lawfully (fairly, according to the rules laid down).
>
> [It is] the hard-working farmer [who labors to produce] who must be the first partaker of the fruits.
>
> Think over these things I am saying [understand them and grasp their application], for the Lord will grant you full insight and understanding in everything.

> Constantly keep in mind Jesus Christ (the Messiah) [as] risen from the dead, [as the prophesied King] descended from David, according to the good news (the Gospel) that I preach. (2 Tim. 2:3–8)

What Qualifies as "Suffering for Jesus"?

You have to honestly be critical of and evaluate your own soil, because different soils have different qualities. Good soil is a mixture of many different properties. It should have clay for water retention, sand for drainage, loam for richness and for holding organic matter, and peat for aeration. In the same way, a human needs a varied input of life components to experience that make up a healthy soil. Christians need to work through trials to build character. That's just the way it is. However, what one views as suffering, another laughs at and says, "I wish that were my problem!"

But let's define, biblically, what suffering through a trial really is. What many religious people consider a trial is really just a reason for them to not move forward. They wallow in the agony of it. Rather than speak to themselves, they listen to themselves. They talk about the mountain with others instead of talking *to* the mountain. When I compare the mountain to God, the ominous threat of it always evaporates. Clearly, I understand that a baby cannot be expected to climb a mountain or make a sandwich from refrigerator ingredients. But that baby is expected to grow up, as in first the blade, then the ear, then the full corn in the ear. You can't stay just a blade. Sometimes life exists on the other side of change. Change is the most consistent thing there is. It can be exciting and full of potential.

> I have a lot more to say about this, but it is hard to get it across to you since you've picked up this bad habit of not listening. By this time you ought to be teachers yourselves, yet here I find you need someone to sit down with you and go over the basics on God again, starting from square one—baby's milk, when you should have been on solid food long ago! Milk is for beginners, inexperienced in God's ways; solid food is for the mature, who have some practice in telling right from wrong. (Heb. 5:11–14 MSG)

The suffering, like a sickness that the devil might throw on you, is not the cross you're to bear. Just as Jesus did 100 percent of the time, you're to stand and say to that mountain, "No! You will not have the victory over me. Sickness, in the name of Jesus, I command you to leave my body!" Say it every day. Say it every day for a year, if that's what it takes. Stand your ground (or "soil," if you will). Here's God's promise:

> With long life will I satisfy him and show him My salvation. (Ps. 91:16 AMPC)

Many say they think God is teaching them something through the sickness. If that's true, then why go to the doctor for help? If God's teaching you, then let Him teach and don't interfere with the lesson by trying to get healthy through the doctor. I thank God for doctors. But as far as learning from God, we already read from 2 Timothy 3:16 that it's the Word that does the teaching. What God wants to teach you is how to read in order to live in His zone.

It's also not suffering as in poverty. Again, I hear people say they don't believe that God wants you prosperous. But these are the same folk who work extra to make more money. Once again, these are lies we tell ourselves. Abraham, Isaac, Jacob, Esau, Joseph, Job, David, Solomon, Jabez, and Jesus Himself (with a treasurer to take care of the money) must have misunderstood God wherever it is that they think He instructed that money is evil and you should stay poor. How do you help others if you remain poor, with only enough for you and yours?

> And Jabez called on the God of Israel, saying, Oh that thou wouldest bless me indeed, and enlarge my coast, and that thine hand might be with me, and that thou wouldest keep me from evil, that it may not grieve me! And God granted him that which he requested. (1 Chron. 4:10 KJV)

Use the Word. I've said it before. Find out what it says. Then become wise. Take care of your body and conduct your finances wisely. Don't abuse yourself in either area. Seek out wise counsel from someone if you need help. But keep after the devil, declaring that he has no legal rights over you. He doesn't. Jesus stripped him of his authority. It's part of the wonderment contained in the power of the name of Jesus.

Biblical suffering is the standing and continuing to stand on the Word of God in the midst of adversity. It's the patience and the discipline you put on yourself in order to polish the *you* that God has created. It's suffering like the Potter refining you in the fiery furnace. It's the tempering process.

> He held seven stars in his right hand, and a sharp double-edged sword came out of his mouth. He looked like the sun shining at its brightest time.
>
> When I saw him, I fell down at his feet like a dead man. He put his right hand on me and said, "Do not be afraid. I am the First and the Last. I am the One who lives; I was dead, but look, I am alive forever and ever! *And I hold the keys to death and to the place of the dead.*" (Rev. 1:16–18 NCV)
>
> Then Jesus came to them and said, "*All power in heaven and on earth is given to me.* So go and make followers of all people in the world. Baptize them in the name of the Father and the Son and the Holy Spirit. Teach them to obey everything that I have taught you, and I will

be with you always, even until the end of this age." (Matt. 28:18–20 NCV)

And these signs shall follow them that believe; In my name shall they cast out devils; they shall speak with new tongues;

They shall take up serpents; and if they drink any deadly thing, it shall not hurt them; they shall lay hands on the sick, and they shall recover.

So then after the Lord had spoken unto them, he was received up into heaven, and sat on the right hand of God.

And they went forth, and preached everywhere, the Lord working with them, and confirming the word with signs following. Amen. (Mark 16:17–20 KJV)

21
Fruit Grown to Perfection

I was a builder and was on a job that needed some concrete poured. I had spoken on the phone with a contractor to help me out with my project, and now I needed to meet up with him to get the plan firmed up. When I called, he didn't pick up, and I found out later that his phone died. On that particular day, I felt the urge to find him. There was a bit of a time crunch, and I needed to get him into my game plan.

I knew the small town where he was currently working and decided to drive there to see if I could find him. It was fifteen miles from home, and whereas I was confident when I left for M-ville, I had twenty minutes to question the decision in my mind. I never said anything out loud to the contrary of my decision. I never voiced the doubt, only the faith. As I approached the exit for M-ville, I thanked God out loud for a good result and asked for His direction, quoting His own principle back to Him.

> Trust in and rely confidently on the Lord with all your heart and do not rely on your own insight or understanding.
>
> In all your ways know and acknowledge and recognize Him, and He will make your paths straight and smooth [removing obstacles that block your way]. (Prov. 3:5–6 AMP)

It wasn't a large town, maybe around 1,500 people. Hopefully, he would be working in the town itself and not in any outlying areas. I drove down Main Street and saw a policeman. I rolled down my window and asked, "Do you know of anyone pouring concrete in the area today?" My thinking was that the policeman gets around and might know. He looked at me in bewilderment with an attitude of, "Why are you wasting my time?" He indignantly said, "*No!* I don't know of anyone."

That didn't boost my confidence. I wish he had said, "No, I don't know, but keep goin', fella! You can do it. You can find him!" In all outward appearance, it looked like I had made a crazy, wrong choice, but God can make crooked ways straight. I said again to myself, "No, God knows where this guy is working. God loves me and is interested in every detail of my life. He will show me the way." So I turned around and took the first right. At the stop sign, there was a man in a pickup truck and I pulled up next to him to ask the same question, "Do you know of a guy in town pouring concrete?" He looked at me with a curious smile and said, "What's his name?" I told him, and he said, "Follow me," and we were off. He was working at this man's home, which was where he was headed! Victory. What a blessing it is! That was exactly how the event happened and how the demand I placed went down. I'll explain the how and why of it in this chapter.

This happened years ago, and yet it has been written down in the annals of my faith history as another amazing miracle God performed on my behalf. I recognized it as nothing less than that, and I rejoiced, then and now, in my salvation. I found my guy and made the needed connection. It was fruit that was grown to perfection, but that's not all.

Here's the harvest I procured: the homeowner in the truck ended up buying thousands of dollars of product from me. And it doesn't end there. He hired me as the construction supervisor over all his building projects. If I had waited for another day, I doubt that I would have met the man at all. Our paths would not have crossed. I would never have been rewarded with God's financial blessing. I knew it. It was fruit to my account. It was a "Jabez" moment (1 Chron. 4:10). I have had countless such unctions on the inside of me similar to this one that produced a harvest for me or, at the very least, saved me trouble.

Just the other day, God told me to ask my wife where my phone was. I wasn't looking for it, but that was what God said to do, so I did. She never takes my phone, but she had inadvertently picked it up and put it in her pocket. She exclaimed, "Oh! I'm sorry! I didn't mean to take it. Were you looking for it long?" Ha! "Not at all," I said. "Not at all."

That's how living in the zone is. It's blessing after blessing, big or small. Here's the thing: just as it charms the parents' heart as they watch as their child opens a wrapped gift, I believe that something like the missing phone episode amuses Jesus's heart. My perception of Jesus is that He chuckles in heaven over such things as we commune with and permit Him to "interfere" with our daily lives.

Read the account given in Luke 5:4–10. I believe Jesus was laughing as their nets broke from the draft of fish caught after Peter informed Him that they had toiled all night and caught nothing.

These events are not coincidence, happenstance, or luck. They represent how I live my life, or try to. If you're a person of faith, they may appear to be miracles. But what seems like a miracle to you and me, God wants to become our everyday life. God says, "This is how *we* do it." For Him it's natural. Only to us is it termed supernatural. God wants us living in His zone, not just sometimes, but all the time.

The thing about the "unavailable concrete guy" event was this: You have to pull down the contrary thoughts as soon as they come in. You can't debate. You can't stand on the shore and dabble your toes in the water, wondering if you should go in. *If* you make the decision to swim, then you have to just dive in.

I remember driving down the road near my house and coming to the stop sign. As I sat for a moment, I thought. If I turned to the right, I would be home. But I turned to the left. I was on my way and had made the decision to go all out. Once you're on your way, don't entertain *any* doubt. Go for it. Just do it.

There was a moment when David said about Goliath, "I'll kill that chump!" There was a moment when Shadrach, Meshach, and Abednego said, "Here's our stand!" You make a decision instantaneously, and then you stand by it. Don't be intimidated by thoughts, doubts, and the like. They'll always be there to shake your confidence in God.

> Shadrach, Meshach, and Abednego, answered and said to the king, O Nebuchadnezzar, we are not careful to answer thee in this matter.
>
> If it be so, our God whom we serve is able to deliver us from the burning fiery furnace, *and he will* deliver us out of thine hand, O king.
>
> But if not, be it known unto thee, O king, that we will not serve thy gods, nor worship the golden image which thou hast set up. (Dan. 3:16–18 KJV)

You choose. Then "let God," as the expression goes. The process is in motion. The seed is in the ground. No farmer yanks up the seed every hour to see if it's sprouted yet.

The process comes *after* the choice. If you engage in the process before the choice (i.e., think it through with options and possibilities, pros and cons, what others will think, negotiations, compromises, and the like), you'll talk yourself right out of the faith you had. Faith is a *now* thing. It's an action word. Most times it is illogical, or it wouldn't be faith. Remember, faith, as God describes it, is like the tiny mustard seed that then grows a huge tree.

An example of the process going first was when Jesus came to his hometown and "he did not many mighty works there because of their unbelief" (Matt. 13:58 KJV). You see, the townspeople had already figured Him out. He was just a carpenter's son, after all—end of story. How could he *possibly* be the Messiah? They'd already made their choice.

> When Jesus had finished telling these stories and illustrations, he left that part of the country. He returned to Nazareth, his hometown. When he taught there in the synagogue, everyone was amazed and said, "Where does he get this wisdom and the power to do miracles?" Then they scoffed, "He's just the carpenter's son, and we know Mary, his mother, and his brothers—James, Joseph, Simon, and Judas. All his sisters live right here among us. Where did he learn all these things?" And they were deeply offended and refused to believe in him.
>
> Then Jesus told them, "A prophet is honored everywhere except in his own hometown and among his own family." And so he did only a few miracles there because of their unbelief. (Matt. 13:53–58 NLT)

In my illustration at the beginning of this chapter, the average person would have waited to get the call through to the concrete contractor and schedule a meeting. But I optimistically decided to place a demand on God and use a different GPS (God's positioning system) and locate him myself, with God's guidance. Is that so crazy? What's the limit of what Jesus can do? The only limits are the ones we place on Him. Listen as Jesus was choosing and gathering his twelve disciples in order to reproduce Himself in them:

> As they approached, Jesus said, "Now here is a genuine son of Israel—a man of complete integrity."

"How do you know about me?" Nathanael asked.

> Jesus replied, "I could see you under the fig tree before Philip found you."
>
> Then Nathanael exclaimed, "Rabbi, you are the Son of God—the King of Israel!"
>
> Jesus asked him, "Do you believe this just because I told you I had seen you under the fig tree? You will see greater things than this." (John 1:47–50 NLT)

Remember in the scriptures when Jesus calmed the sea and the disciples were amazed? They said, "What manner of man is this that even the winds and the sea obey him?" (Matt. 8:27). You know what I think? Whether it was stilling the violent sea or a bunch of fish that shored up his boat and swam it across like Dr. Seuss would have you picture in one of his stories, Jesus was going to get to the other side. When He said, "Let's go," that was it. The choice was made, and that was how it was going to go down! The end.

If you're on the other side of God, might I suggest that you do some more exploring? It's hard to kick a cactus, as the scripture goes (Acts 9:5). If you're an atheist or a nonbeliever at whatever level, be sure of your research because the consequences of making a mistake in this are monumental. If your examination of Christianity and your resulting belief system is based on your own bad life experiences, you have made a mistake. First of all, you can never base your beliefs on experiences—it's an inaccurate system. Secondly, be honest with yourself. There are too many "happenstances and coincidences" to deny God's existence. There's way too much evidence and science in favor of miracles, healings, marvels, and other unexplainable phenomena. Well, unexplainable apart from what the Bible has already said about it.

With my story, I think Jesus was laughing right along with me all the way home from my "find." What I accomplished in boosting my trust in God that day caused me to smile and chuckle as I drove along. If you think this was a gutsy thing to ask for, check out the following three scripture boxes. It wasn't like I asked for the sun to stand still or for there to be no rain for three years. Never doubt what God is willing to perform on your behalf in order to accomplish the desired end.

> And it came to pass, as they fled from before Israel, and were in the going down to Bethhoron, that the Lord cast down great stones from heaven upon them unto Azekah, and they died: they were more which died with hailstones than they whom the children of Israel slew with the sword.

> Then spake Joshua to the Lord in the day when the Lord delivered up the Amorites before the children of Israel, and he said in the sight of Israel, Sun, stand thou still upon Gibeon; and thou, Moon, in the valley of Ajalon.
>
> And the sun stood still, and the moon stayed, until the people had avenged themselves upon their enemies. Is not this written in the book of Jasher [Joshua]? So the sun stood still in the midst of heaven, and hasted not to go down about a whole day.
>
> And there was no day like that before it or after it, that the Lord hearkened unto the voice of a man: for the Lord fought for Israel. (Josh. 10:11–14 KJV)

That was Joshua, Moses's successor. Here's the decree Elijah placed:

> Now Elijah, who was from Tishbe in Gilead, told King Ahab, "As surely as the Lord, the God of Israel, lives—the God I serve—there will be no dew or rain during the next few years until I give the word!" (1 Kings 17:1)

That literally came to pass too. There was drought for three-plus years because of a godly man's command. It doesn't say he conferred with God about it; he commanded it to happen.

Now, before you get crazy on me, I'm not trying to turn you into a magician or to think that God is a genie in a lamp waiting for your rub. I'm trying to get you to stretch your faith in God and get turned on to Him. He loves you and is anxious to show you just how much, if you will turn your passion toward Him the way He has it toward you. Your level of pursuit determines your passion. Know the God whom you serve. Or is the *Late Show* on TV your priority?

> When someone has been given much, much will be required in return; and when someone has been entrusted with much, even more will be required. (Luke 12:48b NLT)

I say this to you, like Jesus asked his soon-to-be apostles (previously termed disciples): "Are you ready to drink of the cup from which I drink?" (Mark 10:39). If you know how those disciples died, you would see how they did indeed follow in His footsteps.

The sun stopping (the real reason for leap year?) and the drought are rather grandiose examples. Here's an example that may be more to our level of thinking—maybe.

> One day the group of prophets came to Elisha and told him, "As you can see,

> this place where we meet with you is too small. Let's go down to the Jordan River, where there are plenty of logs. There we can build a new place for us to meet."
>
> "All right," he told them, "go ahead."
>
> "Please come with us," someone suggested.
>
> "I will," he said. So he went with them.
>
> When they arrived at the Jordan, they began cutting down trees. But as one of them was cutting a tree, his ax head fell into the river. "Oh, sir!" he cried. "It was a borrowed ax!"
>
> "Where did it fall?" the man of God asked. When he showed him the place, Elisha cut a stick and threw it into the water at that spot. Then the ax head floated to the surface. "Grab it," Elisha said. And the man reached out and grabbed it. (2 Kings 6:1–6 NLT)

God cares about the little things that constitute a life. He's got our hairs counted. Currently, with stores on every corner, we may just go buy another ax head to replace the borrowed one, but it wasn't so easy in Elisha's day. Practice your faith every day. Practice your trust in God and in His Word. If you believe it, why wouldn't you?

Back to my story. If I went by my feelings from the time I started until I met up with my goal, I was feeling like this could rank up there as one of the craziest, harebrained ideas I've ever had. But we all know how shaky feelings are. They're like standing at the beach on sand that's rolling out from under your feet after a sea wave comes crashing in.

It rattles your faith when you go by sense knowledge, logic, and what's "normal." God lives and thrives in Miracle Land! He just spoke, and the world was created—and in six days no less. Words. Simple words. Simple faith. That's God's system.

Maybe you've questioned that thing in life you're trying to stand for. Maybe feelings have come in that say, "It's not going to work," "The doctors have said," "I'm never going to break this habit," "He's never going to change," etc. What is faith? It's calling those things that be not as though they are, after all. It's really how God has done everything He's done.

> This happened because Abraham believed in the God who brings the dead back to life and who creates new things out of nothing. (Rom. 4:17b NLT)

When I look back on that day, it wasn't so much the money and it wasn't meeting my guy. It was my lion victory before the Goliath episode. We would never be talking about David without Goliath. And there would never have been any victory for David without the events he had with the lion and the bear.

> And David said to Saul, Let no man's heart fail because of him; thy servant will go and fight with this Philistine.
>
> And Saul said to David, Thou art not able to go against this Philistine to

> fight with him: for thou art but a youth, and he a man of war from his youth.
>
> And David said unto Saul, Thy servant kept his father's sheep, and there came a lion, and a bear and took a lamb out of the flock;
>
> And I went out after him, and smote him, and delivered it out of his mouth; and when he arose against me, I caught him by his beard, and smote him, and slew him.
>
> Thy servant slew both the lion and the bear; and this uncircumcised Philistine shall be as one of them, seeing he hath defied the armies of the living God.
>
> David said moreover, The Lord that delivered me out of the paw of the lion, and out of the paw of the bear, he will deliver me out of the hand of this Philistine. And Saul said unto David, Go, and the Lord be with thee. (1 Sam. 17:32–37 KJV)

Time-out here: We're not reading about the mighty Samson, who was known for his strength and hulk-like build. This is little David. During those many hours of sitting and doing nothing in the pasture, he turned his attention to God and fellowshipped with Him. When the time came and the need arose, God gave Him the equipment needed.

Faith *must* grow. Confidence in God and your relationship with Him must grow. Remember Isaiah 28:10: line upon line, precept upon precept, here a little, there a little. Practice your faith. The biggest and first thing about God is that He needs, requires, and loves to be believed (Heb. 11:6).

My question for you is, How are you working out and growing spiritually? Is your faith a noun or a verb?

> Dear friends, you always followed my instructions when I was with you. And now that I am away, it is even more important. Work hard to show the results of your salvation, obeying God with deep reverence and fear. (Phil. 2:12 NLT)

22

Hidden Fruit

People say, "I'm a Christian," but what I often see is an inebriated, malnourished, depressed, inoperative, ineffective person with their spiritual equipment back in the locker room while they try to play the game of *life*. Tell God you're ready to come off the bench. Get in the game and get your uniform dirty. You'll take some hits and may not score all the time, but you *will* score, and that's worth it all. Victory is sweet!

Daniel knew that hungry lions kill men (Dan. 6.) David knew that Goliath was huge, angry, menacing, and bent on squashing him like a tiny bug (1 Sam. 17). Esther knew she could be killed for going before the king (Esther 4:11). Each one said, "But God…"

Ponder this: How do you think Daniel felt when the king peered in the cave and asked him if he was alive? How do you think David felt *after* the victory over Goliath? Read the book of Esther and the inner struggles she endured. How do you think she felt after sparing the Jewish nation and seeing her wise uncle Mordecai's nemesis killed, resulting in Mordecai being crowned with honor instead?

This is why Paul said in Philippians 4:4, "Rejoice in the Lord always: and again I say rejoice." This is why the Bible says in James 1:2, "Count it all joy," when you come into trouble, because the exercising of your faith is key to true happiness.

I never, never, never, never weigh my problems against my abilities. I weigh them against God and His. I never,

never, never, never voice my doubts. Emotions may rise and thoughts may come, but what I try to say out of my mouth are faith-filled words. I say, "I trust you, God." All I have to do is raise my sail and trust God to blow me through to the other side.

Exercising your faith isn't always about that exact event. Fruit isn't always visible at first. Be open to where that event you're facing will take you. On the way to where you're going, God may detour you to where he really wants you to end up.

David was already picked as king, but nobody knew him. He had little influence (and less respect) even after the prophet Samuel anointed him into this new position. Even King Saul said, "Who's David? Whose son is he?" (1 Sam. 17:55). David was God's pick. He was bringing lunch to his brothers on the battlefront when God planned his formal introduction to the nation of Israel in a big way. I can tell you, there wasn't a soul who *didn't* know David after the Goliath event! Kingship was the position where God wanted him in the first place.

I bought a piece of property once exactly as a result of this principle of "On the way to where you're going."

Just for something different, I was driving the back roads to my destination. I had no particular purpose for taking those roads, although I was always an official "rubbernecker." *Rubbernecking* is a term for those persons who probably don't watch the road as much as they should because they are looking around for interesting "finds." Remember what I told God early in my Christian walk: "Show me what others don't see."

I drove by a country property when God prompted this into my spirit: "There's a house for you." The thing is, I didn't see any house. Thinking I didn't hear correctly, I went about my day. Sometime later, I drove past that piece of property again and got the same prompting yet was confused, not seeing anything there but a driveway leading up to a bunch of trees. After yet a third time, I stopped in the driveway to take a better look. "Ah, so there *is* a house in there!" I said as I observed a gable end peaking above the overgrown trees. Upon closer inspection, behind those tall columnar evergreens was an old two-story farmhouse with white siding. Judging from the deep windowsills, I ascertained that it was constructed of logs. Interestingly, Abraham Lincoln had granted the land when pioneers were heading West and settling forty-acre plots. A tiny log home was constructed and added onto several times as the decades went by, until it became a two-thousand-square-foot all-log home. Perfect for me to renovate.

It was fruit grown for me, kept for me, and timed just right for me to pick. God knows everything and knew I would like it. I asked about it at the nearest residence and, after showing it to my wife, bought it that very evening! The nephew of the now-deceased owner was anxious to sell the house on three acres, and I was able to obtain it for a mere $9,000. God knows.

Fast-forward a bit: We renovated it, lived there for nine years, and sold it for $135,000. It was the only log house I had ever renovated where I was able to retain the logs intact and in place. Every one was in perfect condition. The crazy thing is that when we sold it, the buyer wasn't retired yet and wasn't ready to move in. I didn't have my next log house on the lake built, so I wasn't ready to move out. I rented it back from the buyer for pittance for an additional four years until we were both ready to move. Our realtor said he had never come across such a thing! I truly believe that God orders our steps, if we allow Him to. The whole process could not have worked out better.

So many times we think we are headed toward a goal and the plan is laid out. We're like David happily skipping along, bringing lunch to his brothers on the battlefront, unaware of what's ahead for him/us. We're going to that job interview to get the job. Or like me, we're taking an alternate route to work for no particular reason. In reality, we're proceeding with plan A, unaware that a better plan B will be offered to us. I can tell you that, more often than not, the times I've been surprisingly blessed by something were when I went in a certain direction and an unknown, unplanned blessing popped up. Maybe you don't get the job but you meet someone who contributes greatly to your life. Maybe you find out that you avoided being part of a huge car accident by not taking the normal route to work. The list is unending. Sometimes we never know why plan A didn't work out.

I heard of a woman who got a flat tire on the highway. What an untimely inconvenience! The only thing is, the stranger who stopped to help her later became her husband. Inconvenient, yes, but it sure provided an interesting answer to the question, "How did you meet your spouse?"

We must stop getting irritated (and even angry) with God when things don't go the way we plan. Instead, just thank Him for His presence in the middle of what looks like trouble. Look for things God may have for you. Look for things that are not obvious. Look for fruit that may be hiding behind a leaf or, like my house, hiding behind a *lot* of leaves.

Fruit isn't always highly visible as such. Whatever the case, lay down that mulch. Keep a good attitude. It's imperative. You have *lots* to be thankful for. Nobody wants to bless a brat. Remember, God hates complaining.

> And when the people complained, it displeased the Lord: and the Lord heard it; and his anger was kindled. (Num. 11:1a KJV)

When things go haywire, I've gotten to the point where I'm almost like the guy on a comedy show, looking around for the hidden camera. I'm smiling, saying, "Okay, God, what do you have for me here? What do I need to see that others aren't seeing?" And I can tell you I'm experienced enough in this and have lived long enough on this earth to know that blessing is ahead. He knows He doesn't have to tell me three times anymore before I'll follow His direction. If you'll allow Him to, God will turn that unfortunate-looking event around and bring harvest instead.

Now I truly look forward to the interruptions and detours that God offers. It has given me opportunity to develop my faith. It's sometimes a clear process of calling those things that be not as though they are. You're still speaking, still believing and thinking, but you're allowing God to change the course if need be. Then maybe you can say something like Joseph said to his deceptive, conniving, jealous brothers:

> You intended to harm me, but God intended it all for good. (Gen. 50:20a NLT)

This is going to be most difficult for you, organized plotters, planners, and schedulers. You're going to have to loosen the strings you have on "time" and allow for unscheduled occurrences. Even our American churches have become so regimented and scheduled to the very second of TV time that we give the Holy Spirit no time, and no place, to intervene.

How many times in your life have you ended up like Moses and the children of Israel, with your back up against the Red Sea and the enemy pressing hard? (Exod. 14). Trust me when I tell you we've been there a few times in our lives, my wife and I. With a lot of wandering about the trial, not to mention people who know you doubting your decisions within the trial, you have to stop and "let God." Without knowing it, you're at the perfect place of divine intervention, which can end up as a corner post of your faith life. Like the Hebrews escaping the captivity of Egypt, you may come to remember that event as one of the most important times of your life. While others might complain, you must constantly reframe your thoughts and push on with God. Know that He already has things planned for you.

> "For I know the plans I have for you," says the Lord. "They are plans for good and not for disaster, to give you a future and a hope. In those days when you pray, I will listen. If you look for me wholeheartedly, you will find me. I will be found by you," says the Lord. "I will end your captivity and restore your fortunes. I will gather you out of the nations where I sent you and will bring you home again to your own land." (Jer. 29:11–14 NLT)

This scripture in the box was a promise among many others that God made to the Israelites. But do you know how valuable all of mankind is to Him? This, like so many other scriptures in the Old Testament, is a type and shadow, or a parallel of what He's provided for the Gentiles, for all of us.

God is about progress, growth, and getting that full corn in the ear to maturity and harvested, not so much the little blade poking out of the ground. We must grow and fulfill our destiny, our individual assignments in life. Fulfill the very reason you are made to be on this earth, to show forth the mighty works of God. Like the Israelites, leave off the enslavement in your thinking and be free.

> But you are not like that, for you are a chosen people. You are royal priests, a holy nation, God's very own possession. As a result, you can show others the goodness of God, for he called you out of the darkness into his wonderful light. (1 Pet. 2:9 NLT)

Most people think that seeing is believing, which takes little faith. But the truth is that believing is seeing. Seeing is with the heart, not with the eyes. Again, soil is the heart. The soil says, "I'm going to grow this plant for all I'm worth." That's all it knows. No matter what it looks like, you must believe, as that is seeing for you. You don't necessarily need to see new things; you just need to see with different eyes. See yourself healed. See yourself blessed. See yourself loved. See yourself succeeding. See yourself bold. See yourself secure and confident in the love Jesus brought you.

Would you do me a favor? After you read this next scripture box, would you go sit in a chair for five minutes and ponder on it? (In Hebrew, *Selah*: pause and calmly think of this.) It will bring you to giggles. Ponder this: the moment Mary said yes to the angel, money got up on a camel and started in her direction—hidden fruit to her account.

> Then the angel replied to her, "The Holy Spirit will come upon you, and the power of the Most High will overshadow you [like a cloud]; for that reason the holy (pure, sinless) Child shall be called the Son of God. And listen, even your relative Elizabeth has also conceived a son in her old age; and she who was called barren is now in her sixth month. For with God nothing [is or ever] shall be impossible." Then Mary said, "Behold, I am the servant of the Lord; may it be done to me according to your word." And the angel left her. (Luke 1:35–38 AMPC)

Provision. Help. Fruit. Mary saying yes to God started a whole process in motion. Unlike the Christmas story often portrayed, the wise men (astronomers) did not show up at the stable the night the baby was born. The accurate story is that it took up to two years to reach her, and she probably didn't see any evidence of fruit until they were right in front of her Son, kneeling down and worshipping Him. Fruit came. Not one, not two, but three kings arrived with camels bearing precious gifts. Gold, frankincense, and myrrh—and the gold, according to scholars, was least in value (at that time) of the gifts given. Provision. Help. Fruit. By saying yes, Mary locked into her purpose, her potential, and yes, her fame.

People are depressed because they are working for the wrong thing.

> Therefore do not worry or be anxious (perpetually uneasy, distracted), saying, "What are we going to eat?" or "What are we going to drink?" or "What are we going to wear?"
>
> For the [pagan] Gentiles eagerly seek all these things; [but do not worry,] for your heavenly Father knows that you need them.
>
> But first and most importantly seek (aim at, strive after) Him [His way of doing and being right—the attitude and character of God], and all these things will be given to you also. (Matt. 6:31–33 AMPC)

If you're not living in the zone, the first half of John 10:10 can take over your life.

> The thief comes only in order to steal and kill and destroy. I came that they may have and enjoy life, and have it in

> abundance [to the full, till it overflows]. (John 10:10 AMPC)

Jesus came to bring sight to the blind, and the like, as stated in Isaiah 53. That's what He did. But His mission statement (His purpose) is found at the end of His life as He stood before the governing authorities of the time.

> So Pilate said to Him, "Then you are a King?" Jesus answered, "You say [correctly] that I am a King. This is why I was born, and for this I have come into the world, to testify to the truth. Everyone who is of the truth [who is a friend of the truth and belongs to the truth] hears and listens carefully to My voice." (John 18:37–38 AMPC)

God so desires to reveal truth (Himself, Jesus) to us. It takes work to line yourself up with the principles Jesus taught, but not really. The clash is all in your mind. Train it. Keep your mind clean and pure, filling it with Scripture, and it will fight battles for you. Harvest, in all its varied forms, will come.

> So letting your sinful nature control your mind leads to death. But letting the Spirit control your mind leads to life and peace. (Rom. 8:6 NLT)

23
Harvest

The harvest is wonderful! It's what the planter looks forward to. It's the reaping of the reward of the hard work you've put in.

Many a pig farmer has come in after a hard day's work with the stench of money on his boots. And in your case (the Christian's case), I believe it brings a proud, delighted smile to God when you start using the sickle. That's why Jesus says this in John:

> When you produce much fruit, you are my true disciples. This brings great glory to my Father. (John 15:8 NLT)

God loves it when the harvest is received! He has planned for and prepared for that day when Jesus's followers do something that is only achievable by the faith in God that they utilize. Jesus put up with a lot of suffering in order to harvest us. And He is still harvesting all that we are able to accomplish in His name, since we are now His hands, feet, and mouthpiece.

When people think of the harvest, they instantly think, "What can I get?" Instead, they must think, "What should I be?" You must situate yourself for harvest. And you must realize you are part of a body, so your harvest will be inclusive—for others as well. Actually, you *are* a harvest for some folk. But you can't be the Dead Sea with nothing going out of you. You can't expect to be one who receives but never gives out. It's must be a flow.

> The servant who knows what his master wants but is not ready, or who does not do what the master wants, will be beaten with many blows! But the servant who does not know what his master wants and does things that should be punished will be beaten with few blows. From everyone who has been given much, much will be demanded. And from the one trusted with much, much more will be expected. (Luke 12:47–48 NCV)

When harvest season comes, you should almost hear an alarm go off that says, "I've got to get up and get moving. If I stay here, there will be no harvest." It's a different way of thinking and a different way of seeing.

Remember the farm I worked on as a young man? They were like crazy, busy ants when it was harvesttime. Normal life and regular schedules were set aside during that time. I've worked on farms and have farmer friends. When it's harvesttime, *everything* else takes second place. It's not playtime. Sleep can wait, and even eating. If rain is in the forecast, double shifts and working through the night are on the agenda.

If the devil can get you sidetracked even a little, he can steal your entire harvest. For that day, that week, that portion of your life, you must grab on with all you've got. Timing is everything. All you've done up to this point—the tilling, planting, cultivating, fertilizing, watering, and praying over—has been looking forward to harvest day. You can't let the harvest pass you by. Be ready. Consider this excerpt from E. W. Kenyon's book:

> I Corinthians 3:9, "For we are God's fellow workers; ye are God's husbandry, God's building." The marginal rendering says, "Ye are God's tilled land."
>
> First, you are God's fellow workers. He has called you to labor with Him; so whatever your work is, as long as you are in His will, He is a partner with you. You can't be a failure, for His wisdom is your wisdom; His ability in every department of your life is your ability. All you need to do is to study the Word and get the knowledge that is imparted to you there. Then He will give you the ability to use that knowledge to make your life a success.[4]

For you, the first question is, How is your stalk? The stalk is all about the ability to carry a load. The stalk is to match the load, which is the full corn in the ear.

> The earth produces [acting] by itself—first the blade, then the ear, then the full grain in the ear. But when the grain is

> ripe and permits, immediately he sends forth [the reapers] and puts in the sickle, because the harvest stands ready. (Mark 4:28–29 AMPC)

People want to win the lottery and get millions of dollars, but they have a stalk that is so weak it would bend over with the weight of the fruit. They quickly lose what they have. Look up the statistics of those who have won big money and what they say when it's all over. Most regret, at some level, that it ever happened. Many say they ended up worse than when they started.

In harvest mode, you've got to make sure your machinery is well oiled and in perfect running order. All must be ready. We're looking for peak performance. We want no breakdowns.

> Preach the word [as an official messenger]; be ready when the time is right and even when it is not [keep your sense of urgency, whether the opportunity seems favorable or unfavorable, whether convenient or inconvenient, whether welcome or unwelcome]. (2 Tim. 4:2a AMPC)

Put a seed in the ground and it will do what it's programmed to do, grow. Our part is to acknowledge the rule of seedtime and harvest. What farmer expects a harvest from a field that is not planted? Some people think planting is the hard part—it's not. It's the easy part. But know this: It's never that God is trying to get something from you. It's more that He's trying to get it to us.

> Not that I seek or am eager for [your] gift, but I do seek and am eager for the fruit which increases to your credit [the harvest of blessing that is accumulating to your account]. (Phil. 4:17 AMPC)

I know so many Christians who have no problem sowing, tithing, giving offerings, sending to this mission field and to that one. It's harvesting from that planting that's the hard part for them. Harvest, more than any part of the growth process, has to do with timing.

Of course, you have no harvest if you don't plant. But you also don't have a harvest if you don't develop that blade into a stalk that can produce an ear. We're loaded with people going to church week after week but never developing past the blade stage. Being a churchgoer is not the end-all. Church is a tool. It has many benefits but should never be considered as a replacement of your personal fellowship with the Father. It should enhance living in the zone but never preclude it. Do you know you can become so busy working for God in ministry that you forget Him altogether? His voice can be drowned out by all the clutter of work, no matter what your work/ministry consists.

If honing in to God's voice and His specific direction is a necessity to maintain, here's another tool in the toolshed to keep sharpened for harvest: you must teach yourself to see from your heart first. Selfishness is a problem for those who see only with their eyes. Do you see the needs of others and ask God to help you to help them? Or are you too tied up in your own world? God has no shortage or lack; if you bless someone, God can get you more. He can and will refill your pot. It's no problem for Him. He loves to bless and is in that very business. Jesus said it's more blessed to give than to receive. Giving is one of the most godly things you can do. Tithing and giving financially work to keep your own covetousness and selfishness in check. God is a giver. I've always felt that when I give, for just a moment in time, I can feel what God feels. Who doesn't get that warm, fuzzy feeling inside when they've been obedient to God's prompting to give something to someone?

> For this is how God loved the world: He gave his one and only Son, so that everyone who believes in him will not perish but have eternal life. (John 3:16 NLT)

There are so few people that wear their wealth well. That's why Jesus said it would be difficult for the rich person. Take note: the following teaching from Him first amazed, and then astounded, his disciples.

> Jesus looked around and said to his disciples, "How hard it is for the rich to enter the Kingdom of God!" This amazed them. But Jesus said again, "Dear children, it is very hard to enter the Kingdom of God. In fact, it is easier for a camel to go through the eye of a needle than

> for a rich person to enter the Kingdom of God!"
>
> The disciples were astounded. "Then who in the world can be saved?" they asked. (Mark 10:23–26 NLT)

It's their stalk. It can't hold the load. They get all "twitterpated" with riches. They're enamored by it. They're deceived by its place in their life. I could say much more on the subject. Jesus used many money and/or financial examples in the parables He taught. Money is something all can relate to no matter what century you live in. What's the expression? Money makes the world go around? But money is a tool, that's all—just a tool. It's not a goal. It's not an end. And it's not necessarily a marker of success in life.

Finances aren't the only component of seedtime and harvest. You know the saying, "If you want friends, be friendly. If you want to be loved, show love. If you want respect, give it." You're planting seed. It's the seed-sowing principle in action.

When the Word of God speaks to you, you have to have such a relationship that you're not negotiating or second-guessing and thereby delaying the process. Don't find reasons that today is not the day to harvest. Once you get to know the voice of God, as I've indicated before, it will be heard by a little inner "knowing" or a nudge, but you've got to be in tune. If you're not, you'll miss it. The Holy Spirit will transmit the Father's will to you.

> I have still many things to say to you, but you are not able to bear them or to take them upon you or to grasp them now.

> But when He, the Spirit of Truth (the Truth-giving Spirit) comes, He will guide you into all the Truth (the whole, full Truth). For He will not speak His own message [on His own authority]; but He will tell whatever He hears [from the Father; He will give the message that has been given to Him], and He will announce and declare to you the things that are to come [that will happen in the future].
>
> He will honor and glorify Me, because He will take of (receive, draw upon) what is Mine and will reveal (declare, disclose, transmit) it to you. (John 16:12–14 AMPC)

So the daily question remains, Are we tuned in to what He is transmitting?

I was once at a job and was awakened by God in the middle of the night. I felt an unshakable need to speak some words, from Him, to the manager of this very old elegant hotel in the downtown of the city I was in. He was a young man and had only been on the job about a year. I'll call him Victor for the sake of anonymity. Victor always wore a suit, if that helps you visualize his authority at this hotel with hundreds of employees under his supervision.

The nudging didn't dissipate in the morning when I got up. I knew it was from God and that I would have to speak what He had told me the previous night. There was no shaking the "knowing" of what I had to do. It's always a bit of an awkward thing, you know, when you're not fully informed as to the why of things. God knows. And the one you speak to knows. You're the only one in the dark. You're just the messenger. But someone's harvest may be at stake, so you better hear accurately and do exactly as instructed.

I knew Victor took a certain elevator when he came in at 8:00 a.m. Indeed, I found him as he entered that morning and asked if I could speak with him. (Timing. Remember the urgency of harvest? I had a very busy day ahead, but God takes precedence, especially when harvest is at hand.) I made small talk until we reached his office, entered, sat down, and got settled. Then I told him I had something to say to him from God. Of course, I didn't even know if he was a believer. But he got serious, reached behind him, and pushed a button that automatically closed his door. It was out there—I couldn't change horses in the middle of this stream now.

I told him exactly what God told me, no more, no less. God's message to Victor was twofold. I started with telling him that God was very pleased with him and that he should hold to his integrity. I stated, "Whatever you're in the middle of, you don't have to worry. Your character will carry you through." I also told Victor that God said he didn't necessarily need all the rituals with his children but just to place their hands in God's hand. I ended with, "I'm only telling you what God told me." That was it. My message was delivered.

He stared at me with a most penetrating look. I didn't know what he was thinking. Did the words I was so sure of strike a nerve? Was he considering throwing me out of his office?

Finally, he said, "That's very interesting." I didn't even know if he had a family, so I was somewhat relieved when he said he was Catholic and that he was doing his best to teach his sons to have faith in God.

The next morning, he saw me and said, "Can you come talk with me?" We went to his office.

He started with, "You didn't know this yesterday," and he told me what had transpired over the last two days. Apparently, there was a venue booking Victor had done of some entertainment for the hotel. But the governing board wanted another group in that time slot instead, so they asked him to make the change. Victor boldly affirmed with them that he had given his word to the first group and therefore could not make the change. The board told him to seriously reconsider his answer to them. They stated plainly, "We're the ones who hired you. Just make something up and cancel it." The battle was on.

Well, with the confirmation I had given him from God to hold to his integrity, how could he have any other answer for the board than the one he had already given? The prior morning, when I had given him that Word from God, I'm sure he was on pins and needles, as a follow-up meeting with his bosses was to ensue. Maybe that was the reason for the blank stare after my message to him? Maybe he was trying to gauge if somehow I had some inside information, which I did, just not from a human source.

At any rate, the board held their meeting with him and apologized! They said, "We're sorry that we asked you to do this. Your honesty and character is the very thing we hired you for." The short of it is, his job was saved, and his relationship with the board was bettered because of the "crisis." Harvest.

As for me? It was funny what happened before I left there on that particular trip. I was outside by the valets, waiting to have my car brought up, when a young valet said to me, "You look like a wise man who might be able to help me with a problem." This came out of the blue. What? Who, me? While he was asking his question, his boss, Victor, came up from behind and told the valet, "I don't know what you two are talking about, but you should take heed to whatever this man has to say to you!" Victor and I exchanged glances and an appreciative, in-the-know smile. I hoped my advice to the young man was right on.

Operating in the zone—it's boundless and is always the best place to operate from. For harvest in God's kingdom, remember you have to be ready in season and out.

We have to look at harvest in all its varied forms. You plant all kinds of seeds in your life. That's why it's important to plant only good ones! A seed only produces after its kind. You never pick a tomato from a cornstalk. The fruit from a plant will be what's programmed into the seed. God must have heard Victor's prayers from the heart. Victor must have planted seeds of good character in his life to have such a confirmation from God *and* from his bosses. These are promotions you can't buy with money. They only come through the exercise of who you really are, based on what you've planted. Anybody can say they're a great drummer, but when you're given two sticks and a snare, how does it sound? Victor probably sounded great on his résumé, but now they truly knew he was who he said he was. I'm sure he indeed enjoyed the harvest that day.

Harvest. That's what it was for me, too, yet in a different form. Whenever I'm in that city, that extravagant, classy, opulent, marble-floored hotel is my host. I get shown great favor, if you know what I mean. Even when I was there doing my job, my crew and I were allowed to stay in the hotel, much to the dismay of the project manager over me, who said that *never* happens. Favor. Godly favor. There's nothing like it. It puts a smile in your heart and makes you confirm to yourself, "I truly have friends in high places."

> And Jesus went about all the cities and villages, teaching in their synagogues, and preaching the gospel of the kingdom, and healing every sickness and every disease among the people.
>
> But when he saw the multitudes, he was moved with compassion on them, because they fainted, and were scattered abroad, as sheep having no shepherd.
>
> Then saith he unto his disciples, The harvest truly is plenteous, but the labourers are few;
>
> Pray ye therefore the Lord of the harvest, that he will send forth labourers into his harvest. (Matt. 9:35–38 KJV)

God declared to me some time ago that if I would speak to whomever He directed me without any negotiation, no matter how awkward, He would "keep my pot filled." Now some may ask, "Pot at the end of a rainbow?" Although physical and spiritual both apply, the scripture that came to mind at that time was 2 Kings 4:1–7. That discourse is about a woman facing financial ruin. She goes to the prophet Elisha for help. He instructs her to take the only available resource she has, a small pot of oil. She is to borrow every available empty pot from her neighbors. The prophet then has her pour from her vessel of oil into the others and keep on pouring, until every single one has been filled. In that way, her financial worries were taken care of. The oil was hers to sell. God created income for her.

God has been true to His Word to me! He keeps my pot filled. For example, once, I was out of town and loading a semi with goods to bring home to sell. I've done a lot of liquidating in my life. It's part of my personal gifting. (Remember, I'm always looking for what others don't see. Many times, I see the value in things that others overlook.) I had hired local help for the day and had about eight guys working hard all morning, lifting and loading by hand. I had promised them lunch. I knew at the moment of that decision that God wanted me to speak to one particular guy. I motioned for him to come with me to a fast-food restaurant and help me with the food and drink.

As he got into my vehicle, I emptied my pocket of a wad of cash and put it into the center console. It was wrapped on the outside with a few hundreds, which I noticed made him raise his eyebrows. I noticed his gaze and asked him, "Would you like to know how to get that kind of cash?" He answered excitedly, "Yeah!"

I stated seriously, "Okay, I will tell you the secret, but you have to be completely honest with me first." Looking at him straight on, I told him that in this moment of time in our lives, I only had fifteen minutes alone with him and that God had expressly told me to talk to him. I proceeded to jump into the middle of his life. I hit him with both barrels, as the expression goes.

I asked if he was doing drugs. Yes. Stealing? Yes. Girls? Yes. I said plainly with confidence, "Yep, that will never bring you true joy. You'll be left feeling empty every night, living a life like that." Then I said, "Here's the secret: keep God in the middle of everything you do. If you do, if you live your life God's way, you'll feel fulfilled and happy at the end of each day instead of purposeless and dissatisfied, always wanting but not able to obtain."

He looked a little more surprised. He was quiet for ten seconds or so. Then he told me that he had committed his life to Jesus when he was nine years old but had veered away.

We were just pulling up to the intercom to place the order when he slapped the dash with both hands. Now *I* was the surprised one. He declared loudly, "Well, I never thought my day was going to go like this when I woke up this morning!" He then answered fervently to my question, "Yes, I would like to pray to recommit my life to Jesus!"

I told the girl on the other end of the intercom, "Can you wait just one minute to take my order?" and I prayed out loud with the guy to devote his life to Christ.

When I pulled up to pick up my nine burger meals, the girl at the window turned around and yelled, "Hey, this is the guy!" The manager and another worker showed up at the window. Apparently, my prayer was on speaker and they wanted to greet us and shake our hands. Harvest should and *will* bless others.

On the way back to the semi, I gave him some more instructions on living life successfully. Then I concluded with a statement that went something like this: "You watch. You keep an eye on me this afternoon. In some way, somehow, God is going to bless me." That was a bold, prophetic statement, I know. But it was harvesttime, and I knew it. God was about to fill my pot beyond my expectations for that particular job.

As we continued to load the semi, the manager of the establishment came out and asked me if I could fit some patio furniture onto the truck. I had already eyed it up previously that day. It was some great, valuable furniture! He had changed his mind and decided to get rid of it. Did I want it? You bet. It was well worth its space on the truck. However, as it was gathered at the back to be loaded, the project manager for the job (my boss or, more accurately, the one who had contracted me) came along. He had been easy to work with and particularly helpful to me on this job. He showed great interest in the patio furniture. I said, "Do you like it? Do you want it?" He heartily said yes, so I sacrificed my "prize" harvest. Or did I?

The project manager came back a little while later that afternoon and announced, as he pointed to a forty-foot container there in the parking lot, "Whatever is in that container is yours." What was behind door number 2? Multiple thousands of dollars' worth of unused, brand-new product! He knew exactly what was in there. It was part of his jobsite cleanup to get rid of it. It was many times larger in value than the nice patio furniture.

I looked up and caught the eye of the worker watching the whole event as it transpired that afternoon. He was shaking his head in wonderment and smiling one of the biggest white-teeth smiles I'd ever seen. Harvest is wonderful. It brings great joy.

You have to learn to let things and money go *through you*. Sometimes trying to hang on to too much at one time will cause you trouble. It's like a cat with each paw on a mouse when another runs under his nose. What will he do? He may lose all in his attempt to get what else is "out there." It's the same for people who have been blessed with a great spouse or family or house or job. Can their character last throughout, or will they self-sabotage their own blessings in life? Will their stalk succumb under the weight of God's goodness toward them? The harvest.

There's a fine line between harvesting and hoarding. It's easy to trick yourself into thinking, "Oh, I need this or I need more." The transaction of a person who sees a need and gives toward it (especially out of their own need) is as beautiful as a flower. God said this to me one afternoon: "To be stingy is to be crippled. To be greedy is to be ugly. To see with your eyes only is to be blind. To be a giver is to be beautiful. To be unselfish is to run like a deer. And to see with your heart is the clarity of life itself."

There is something inside of us that we can tap into. We are God's wonderful harvest. We are amazing, way more than normal or just average. But living by the Spirit really goes against our senses and our experiences. And it goes against the way the world operates. The Holy Spirit is our teacher and guide. And Jesus is our example.

> So the Word became human and made his home among us. He was full of unfailing love and faithfulness. And we have seen his glory, the glory of the Father's one and only Son. (John 1:14 NLT)

24
The Conclusion

My dad died when I was fifteen. After that, I was getting into trouble, so I was moved out of my home in the suburbs to live in the country with an older brother and his family. I wasn't happy about the move and expressed it in numerous ways. I painted my room black and maintained the same distrust for grown-ups that I had had in my younger years.

One day, as I sat on the hill overlooking the farm, I had this thought: *This world couldn't have happened accidentally. There has to be a Creator.* Later that night, as I lay in bed, I said this prayer: "God, I don't even know if You're really there, but if You are, I want You to come into my life and help me to be different."

If any person heard that prayer, they might have thought it to be quite useless. It seemed like I had dialed God's number before and never got an answer. This time, however, I was ready. My heart attitude was correct. I was desperate to have the God-size void filled in my life. The prayer was effectual. I slept that night with a peace and contentment that I had never felt before. I had taken a turn. I didn't know where I was headed, but my hope was that it would be better.

I felt different on the inside. God was starting to work in me, as far as I allowed him to, that is. The only thing I knew was the peace I felt after I called on Him. I know now it's the commitment to God that counts. That's what He's looking for. It's nothing to just believe in God. Even demons believe in, *and fear*, God. The Bible says this:

> Thou believest that there is one God; thou doest well: the devils also believe, and tremble. (James 2:19 KJV)

I had a lot of rough edges to smooth out. A lot! The first day at my new high school, I witnessed two bigger kids at the front door picking on a freshman. My old nature kicked in. I decked both bullies and, with hardly a missed step in my stride, entered the door. That exchange also made my presence known in the small school. My message was that I was not to be trifled with. At that time in my life, my street smarts took precedence over the Holy Spirit's guidance and wisdom.

The way I see it now, the same black-and-white view I had as a young person carried through to my early Christian walk. My feeling was, if you're God's enemy, then you're mine.

There weren't any shades of gray there for me. My friends got me a T-shirt years ago that expressed their perception of me and the way I see the Word of God. Embossed in gold on the front was a picture of the Bible, and on the back it said, "Just Do It."

When referring to God's Word, there are two Greek words for *word* found in the Bible, *Logos* and *Rhema*. *Logos* is the Written Word; it is the Bible. It's the God-inspired, given-to-mankind revelation of how our world operates—its history and its future. It details people who have lived before and what they did in their lives, right or wrong. And let me say, just because you read about someone in the Bible doesn't mean you are to emulate what he or she did. All scripture needs to be read in the light of other scripture. Thus, it creates an accurate picture of correct doctrine to follow. Don't ever hang your hat on one particular scripture unless it's balanced with others.

Rhema is more the God-breathed-into-your-spirit Word from God. It's specific for the occasion or need that you're facing, or for what someone else is facing. It's that voice directly from God spoken to you, felt deep down in your "knower." It's the voice you're to get to know.

> The sheep that are My own hear *and* are listening to My voice; and I know them, and they follow Me. (John 10:27 AMPC)

Jesus didn't promise he would do away with hardship in your life, just that you would have peace and a solution in the midst of it. He always has a way for you to make it through to the other side. No, the easy life is not His aim, but the victorious life is. And within that, it's essential to know the Logos Word in order to hear the Rhema Word from God and live life in the zone.

I've worked at understanding the Written Word. I have a desire to help people, thus the book. I still support the underdogs, those struggling in life. I may not be the one to go to if you're looking for consolation in your pain. I may cut it short if you attempt to cry on my shoulder, because I'm anxious to get you to the solution for your pain. If you're a bully, I won't hold you down with my fist in your throat and demand you accept the wonderful salvation God has for you. Those days are long gone, but my fervor is still there. I've tempered my approach and methods of dealing with people, but my desired end result is the same. The zeal from which I operate now, both for myself and for others, is to grow the stalk strong in order to hold the full corn in the ear in every area.

On the enemy's side, the storm's ultimate goal is to stop you from producing or at least to delay your harvest. If he's able, he has another day to devise a plan to wreck your world. The scheme is to keep you in your past and your wrong thinking. Lies, deception, and the like are hoping to keep you at the blade stage. Consider this scripture:

> Don't be misled—you cannot mock the justice of God. You will always harvest what you plant. Those who live only to satisfy their own sinful nature will harvest decay and death from that sinful nature. But those who live to please the Spirit will harvest everlasting life from the Spirit. So let's not get tired of doing

> what is good. At just the right time we will reap a harvest of blessing if we don't give up. (Gal. 6:7–9 NLT)

God is interested in the harvest: the fruit to perfection, your character blossoming with peace, love, joy, etc.

> But the fruit of the [Holy] Spirit [the work which His presence within accomplishes] is love, joy (gladness), peace, patience (an even temper, forbearance), kindness, goodness (benevolence), faithfulness, gentleness (meekness, humility), self-control (self-restraint, continence). Against such things there is no law [that can bring a charge]. (Gal. 5:22–23 AMPC)

Serving God wasn't my objective in my early years at the small country college I attended, but at one point in my sophomore year, I was invited to go to a church in the city. This church was downtown on a street known to be in the heart of the red-light district. The one or two thousand members met together in a building that was an old elaborate theater complete with tall red velvet curtains. On Saturday nights, the sidewalk in front carried prostitutes and drug dealers. On Sunday mornings, it carried Bible-enraptured believers. We walked past the leftovers from the night before to enter into a radical, exuberant, Spirit-filled environment of doers of the Word. That was very new to me, considering my very conservative church background, but I found it drawing more than just my curiosity. It was the first church where I ever saw people truly happy and free enough to show it.

I still remember viewing my first miraculous healing there. Skeptical, I had placed myself on the front row of this faith healer's "performance." He prayed for a man's leg to grow out to be equal to the other. I wanted to see the instant replay, but there was none. I had seen the man limp onto the stage without the lift in his shoe. One leg was dramatically shorter than the other, and that leg grew out! I've never forgotten it. God is real. And God cares. That man was one happy fellow as he exited the platform. I imagine it was just like the guy in this scripture:

> Then Peter took the lame man by the right hand and helped him up. And as he did, the man's feet and ankles were instantly healed and strengthened. He jumped up, stood on his feet, and began to walk! Then, walking, leaping, and praising God, he went into the Temple with them. (Acts 3:7–8 NLT)

The church was a good distance from my college dorm, forty-five minutes to an hour away. I remember driving home and crossing the big bridge after being filled with the Spirit of God, praying in my newly acquired tongue. The devil tempted me with thoughts like, "Now you've really gone over the edge. Now you're downright crazy!" But I stuck with God and my newfound power, which I knew nothing about, yet. Here's what happened that night and the very next day. God is my witness. This is the truth just as it occurred.

I arrived home late, maybe at midnight. I had a test the next day to study for. As I opened up the textbook at my desk, I heard a knock on my door. It was a guy I had seen around. Why he came to me, I still have no clue. He said his dad was a pastor, that he was hypnotizing people to quit smoking, and did I think that was right? He wanted to have a Bible study with me to find out. I agreed to it, and we went down the hall to a small meeting room.

We were still at it a couple of hours later when the downtown bars closed and a number of guys walked by, asking what we were doing. Some asked if they could join us. I didn't get much sleep that night, and I hadn't studied at all for that test. I hadn't been the greatest student. In truth, I had never even opened the textbook all quarter long. I asked God to help me. I remembered, at the church they told me I was now filled with Holy Ghost's power and to ask God for direction and help. I literally flipped through the pages of the book and read sentences from here and there.

In class the next morning, every sentence I had read from the book was a test question! That was one of the few *As* I received at the university. I came home from class and leaned against a huge tree in front of my dorm, pondering what just happened in that classroom and the night before. I thought, *So this is what it feels like to have the right answers!*

I have visited that same tree a number of times in my life since that day.

As I stood there contemplating, a college kid came up to me and asked if I knew how to get "born again." "What? Why are you asking *me*?" I said. He answered, "I don't know. You just look like you would know." I began quoting scriptures to him that I didn't even know I knew! It was amazing both to me and to him. I'll never forget that first experience of tapping into the real power of God. I saw God do things for me, with me, around me, about me, including me, and in spite of me, like I had never seen before. It was euphoric, like no high I had ever been on.

That got me. I was glued. My wagon was hooked to God's for life. I might not have straightened up my act right away, but little by little I worked out my salvation. The chaff was blowing off and away from my wheat.

> The prophet that hath a dream, let him tell a dream; and he that hath my word, let him speak my word faithfully. What is the chaff to the wheat? saith the Lord.
>
> Is not my word like as a fire? saith the Lord; and like a hammer that breaketh the rock in pieces? (Jer. 23:28–29 KJV)

While we were dating in college, my wife remembers me telling her, "God's got a call on my life." And surely he did, as he does for everyone who will listen with attentive ears. I truly had a great future ahead. God has thoroughly changed me from the inside out.

> "For I know the plans I have for you," says the Lord. "They are plans for good and not for disaster, to give you a future and a hope." (Jer. 29:11 NLT)

Are you frustrated in life? Tired of working only to be disappointed? Are you dried up inside? Turn in His direction. Sometimes you have to exfoliate your own thinking and put on some Holy Spirit oil.

> Thou lovest righteousness, and hatest wickedness: therefore God, thy God, hath anointed thee with the *oil* of gladness above thy fellows. (Ps. 45:7; Heb. 1:9 KJV)

Understand this: for God, we are that treasure buried in the field, or that pearl of great price the merchant gave everything he had to obtain (Matt. 13:44–46). We are the prize. When you get the revelation of what that means, healing is not a problem. Provision has no hindrance, neither in your thinking nor in actuality. The devil has no hold on you. You can go as far with God as you choose to go. You can receive it all, or you can cut out pages and parts of the Bible that are too hard for you to accept. It is, indeed, your choice.

When you find a treasure, you analyze, "What is it going to take to get this?" So questions come up, like, "To be a Christian, I have to *what*?" People have one hundred thousand ideas and opinions about *everything*. Water's free. It's the best drink there is, but we purchase all kinds of other water-based drinks that are the worst for us. We want flavor, taste, and rich aroma. In America, we'll drive fifteen minutes to go out to breakfast because we like the coffee they serve, yet we skip over the imperative in life. Obtaining truth is the imperative.

Before you move forward, you have to make distinctions between what seems true and what is 100 percent true, because a half-truth is still a lie. Just because everybody agrees with it doesn't make it true. You must find out for yourself, or you may be deceived, which will not turn out well for you. When you're deceived, you're deceived. You can't see it. That's the very nature of deception. We do love to lie to ourselves.

> The prudent understand where they are going, but fools deceive themselves. (Prov. 14:8 NLT)

The Word is truth. You, as a person, *are* what Jesus died for. And if He was willing to pay everything for *you*, do you think he might be willing to pay a little for your well-being? Your health? Your prosperity? Your sanity? It's so simple. It skips over all the questions of, "Is the Bible true?" All the TV programs and movies that "interpret" the Bible can be deceptive and take you away captive. You better find out for yourself.

> The message of the cross is foolish to those who are headed for destruction! But we who are being saved know it is the very power of God. (1 Cor. 1:18 NLT)
>
> For the wisdom of this world is foolishness to God. As the Scriptures say, "He traps the wise in the snare of their own cleverness." (1 Cor. 3:19 NLT)

Don't be deceived—in anything. Sit on a hill, observing nature and its impeccable majesty. Contemplate the various unexplainable miracles you've heard of over the years. Movies have even been made about them. Maybe the evening news has carried the story of an unexplainable, nonscientific event. There are hundreds of thousands of testimonies even from our lifetime that defy the science that would try to falsify them. The Bible says this:

> Jesus also did many other things. If they were all written down, I suppose the

> whole world could not contain the books that would be written. (John 21:25 NLT)

Open your ears and your hearts. Doubt arises because you see with your eyes only. I've always said, "It takes a lot of faith to be an atheist." You must really have to grasp at straws to believe there is no God. Yes, that takes great faith, considering all the things we encounter in this world that point in His direction.

Believing God is easy. By the way, the answer to the hypnosis question we arrived at was this: if it's not contained in the Bible, as in Jesus or God being our example and doing it, it's out of bounds. Steer clear of it. There are a lot of counterfeits to faith out there. And don't forget this scripture:

> For whatsoever is not of faith is sin. (Rom. 14:23b KJV)

I smoked for nine years as a young person. God never told me I had to quit. He just said, "Every time you take a puff, raise it up to Me and say, 'This one's for you, Lord.'" That put a new spin on it for me. I took my last puff shortly thereafter.

Don't stress about things you can't possibly know the answer to or are supposed to. But you also can't be like Little Red Riding Hood skipping along through life not aware of a big bad wolf roaming around, looking for folks weak in faith.

> Be sober, be vigilant; because your adversary the devil, as a roaring lion, walketh

> about, seeking whom he may devour. (1 Pet. 5:8 KJV)

Neither ignoring the devil nor trying to outsmart him has ever been the Christian's mandate. We only use the Word against him. We speak. That's our weaponry.

> (For the weapons of our warfare are not carnal, but mighty through God to the pulling down of strong holds;)
>
> Casting down imaginations, and every high thing that exalteth itself against the knowledge of God, and bringing into captivity every thought to the obedience of Christ. (2 Cor. 10:4–5 KJV)

The Bible recounts victorious events that begin with such expressions as, "He said…," God said…," "Jesus said…," "The centurion said…," "She said within herself…," and "Say to this mountain…" Words are how God has set up our world and has done everything that He has done. And it's His instruction to us to use that same powerful force.

Whole wars have been started with words. Terrible grievances have been forgiven by words. Arguments have been stopped by words. God introduced the second Adam, Jesus, His Son, with words by saying this:

> While he yet spake, behold, a bright cloud overshadowed them: and behold a

> voice out of the cloud, which said, This is my beloved Son, in whom I am well pleased; hear ye him. (Matt. 17:5 KJV)

Everyone who has ever made a difference in the world (who we still talk about today) was because of his or her words. Don't misfire with your words. Aim, shoot, and hit the bull's-eye. Whatever you need, it's there.

Studies have been done as to what people go through when they're left alone with only their thoughts. How do they react with no other people to talk to, no phone, no TV, no radio, and no books, with no input from any outside source? Most don't like it, and some go insane, unable to direct their own thoughts. At this point in my life, I don't know what I would do if I *couldn't* just sit in a chair and commune with God. I've formed such a habit of consulting His direction for my everyday life that it makes me uncomfortable to try to move out on my own volition.

One of the most fruitful things my wife and I have "discovered" is praying together every morning. I don't mean I pray something and then she prays something and we say "Amen" to each other's prayer; I mean, I pray a line and then she says the exact same thing. Sometimes she leads in prayer. If a prayer is going to be in agreement, then you have to be saying the same things.

> Again I say unto you, That if two of you shall agree on earth as touching any thing that they shall ask, it shall be done for them of my Father which is in heaven. (Matt. 18:19 KJV)

The definition of the word *agreement* is "consistency; harmony or accordance in opinion or feeling; the absence of incompatibility between two things; the act of coming to a mutual decision." The Father, the Son, and the Holy Spirit are in complete agreement with one another. They back one another. What the Father says to say, they say. What the Father says do, they do. We've read scripture on that before.

If you're not married, find someone to pray with. It's powerful. It seems too simple to be effective, and yet compared to other means of prayer, I don't know if I can accurately express to you how fruitful praying together in agreement has been for us. It's like the redwood tree compared to the white pine. It's like the fiery, dancing flames of the aurora borealis compared to a quick flash of lightning. It's rich, and it's effective.

There's so much more to life—everyone's life. Find out. I can't myself imagine where I go from here, but I know it's going to be magnificent!

I've only scratched the surface of what it means to hear the voice of God. It will be your job to explore living life in the zone and what that means for you. Just like you have your own DNA, fingerprint, and voiceprint, your fellowship with God will be different from anyone else's.

Our prayer is that you take the time to explore the zone. I can guarantee, you won't ever be the same once you taste and see that the Lord is good (Ps. 34:8). This is the start to whet your appetite, this book and this scripture passage:

> You'll remember, friends, that when I first came to you to let you in on God's master stroke, I didn't try to impress you with polished speeches and the latest phi-

losophy. I deliberately kept it plain and simple: first Jesus and who he is; then Jesus and what he did—Jesus crucified.

I was unsure of how to go about this, and felt totally inadequate—I was scared to death, if you want the truth of it—and so nothing I said could have impressed you or anyone else. But the Message came through anyway. God's Spirit and God's power did it, which made it clear that your life of faith is a response to God's power, not to some fancy mental or emotional footwork by me or anyone else.

We, of course, have plenty of wisdom to pass on to you once you get your feet on firm spiritual ground, but it's not popular wisdom, the fashionable wisdom of high-priced experts that will be out-of-date in a year or so. God's wisdom is something mysterious that goes deep into the interior of his purposes. You don't find it lying around on the surface. It's not the latest message, but more like the oldest—what God determined as the way to bring out his best in us, long before we ever arrived on the scene. The experts of our day haven't a clue about what this eternal plan is. If they had, they wouldn't have killed the Master of the God-designed life on a cross. That's why we have this Scripture text:

No one's ever seen or heard anything like this,
Never so much as imagined anything quite like it—
What God has arranged for those who love him.

But *you've* seen and heard it because God by his Spirit has brought it all out into the open before you.

The Spirit, not content to flit around on the surface, dives into the depths of God, and brings out what God planned all along. Who ever knows what you're thinking and planning except you yourself? The same with God—except that he not only knows what he's thinking, but he lets *us* in on it. God offers a full report on the gifts of life and salvation that he is giving us. We don't have to rely on the world's guesses and opinions. We didn't learn this by reading books or going to school; we learned it from God, who taught us person-to-person through Jesus, and we're passing it on to you in the same firsthand, personal way.

The unspiritual self, just as it is by nature, can't receive the gifts of God's Spirit. There's no capacity for them. They seem like so much silliness. Spirit can be known only by spirit—God's Spirit and our spirits in open communion. Spiritually alive, we have access to everything God's Spirit is doing, and can't be judged by unspiritual critics. Isaiah's question, "Is there anyone around who knows God's Spirit, anyone who knows what he is doing?" has been answered: Christ knows, and we have Christ's Spirit. (1 Cor. 2 MSG)

Epilogue

Living in the Zone is like sitting on the edge of your seat anticipating what might happen next in a thrilling action movie. The amazing thing is that you're the star in that movie.

The zone is more fun than you can ever imagine. It will produce more than any job that you've ever loved and succeeded in. It creates a knowing that your life truly has purpose.

Operating from the zone will give you the best vehicle to drive through life until you see Him face-to-face.

Here's to the "whoever" ones who dare to pursue God and take on the challenge of following the peculiar leading of the Spirit of God in their life, listening for that voice in the inner man.

Appendix

Recommended Reading

Any book by E. W. Kenyon:

The Bible in the Light of Our Redemption
In His Presence
New Creation Realities
The Hidden Man: An Unveiling of the Subconscious Mind
The Power of Your Words
The Blood Covenant

Books by Kenneth E. Hagin:

The Holy Spirit and His Gifts
Bible Faith Study Course
Bible Prayer Study Course

Other Books:

Seven Deadly Emotions, by Don Colbert
Who Switched off my Brain? by Carolyn Leaf
How God Changes Your Brain, by Andrew Newberg, MD, and Mark Robert Waldman
Change Your Brain, Change Your Life, by Daniel G. Amen, MD
Healing the Broken Brain, by Eldon Chalmers
Grown-up Children, Childhood Pain, by Dr. Paul Hegstrom
My Journey With God, by Wellington Boone
God's Generals, by Roberts Liardon
Maximizing Your Potential, by Dr. Myles Monroe
The Power of Positive Thinking, by Norman Vincent Peale

Battlefield of the Mind, by Joyce Meyer
George Washington Carver, In His Own Words, edited by Gary R. Kremer

Notes

1 Andrew Newberg, MD, and Mark Robert Waldman, *How God Changes Your Brain* (New York: Ballantine Books Trade Paperbacks, a division of Random House Inc., 2009), 163.

2 Janet and Geoff Benge, *Heroes of Faith, George Washington Carver—From Slave to Scientist* (Lynwood, WA: Emerald Books, 2001), 159–163.

3 Eldon Chalmers, *Healing the Broken Brain* (Coldwater, MI: Remnant Publications, 1998), 41.

4 E. W. Kenyon, *Advanced Bible Course* (Lynnwood, WA: Kenyon's Gospel Publishing Society, 1970), 55.

About the Authors

Dan and Suzi have been married for over forty years at the publication of this book. In that time, they've learned some extraordinary things.

Dan always says Bible school for him was completed in the six years they lived without electricity and running water. Because there really wasn't much to do in the evenings under the light of a single Aladdin lamp, it resulted in the subsequent study of the Word, and Dan's hunger for God grew.

Desiring to stay out of debt as they built their first log home together, they trusted God every step of the way. Many times, they placed themselves in difficult situations, by choice. Such a thing helps you find out who you are and also who you can be. From such learning, they built their home with almost no money, started a church and pastored it for twenty years, built a nearly impossible thirty-thousand-square-foot mansion for someone, and taught of God's goodness the entire time. For them, it has been lives well spent. And still their declaration is, "The best is yet to come!"